THE

ART

OF

LIVING

D1113978

THE ART OF

Living

Thoughts on Meeting

the Challenge of Life

Wilferd Peterson

BRISTOL
PARK
BOOKS

Previously published in three separate volumes as
The Art of Living copyright © 1960, 1961
by Wilferd A. Peterson
The New Book of the Art of Living copyright © 1962, 1963
by Wilferd A. Peterson
More about the Art of Living copyright © 1966
by Wilferd A. Peterson
Quotation from *The Art Spirit* by Robert Henri reprinted
by permission of J.B. Lippincott Company

First Bristol Park Books edition published in 1997.

Bristol Park Books
A division of Budget Book Service, Inc.
386 Park Avenue South
New York, NY 10016

Bristol Park Books is a registered trademark
of Budget Book Service, Inc.

Published by arrangement with Heacock Literary Agency, Inc.

Library of Congress Catalog Card Number: 97-70024
ISBN: 0-88486-159-7

Printed in the United States of America.

Contents

~~~~

Art when really understood is the province of every human being.

It is simply a question of doing things, anything, well. It is not an outside extra thing.

When the artist is alive in any person, whatever his kind of work may be, he becomes an inventive, searching, daring, self-expressing creature. He becomes interesting to other people. He disturbs, upsets, enlightens, and he opens ways for a better understanding.

—ROBERT HENRI
in *The Art Spirit*

THE ART OF
Achievement

You hold in your hand the camel's-hair brush of a painter of Life. You stand before the vast white canvas of Time. The paints are your thoughts, emotions and acts.

You select the colors of your thoughts; drab or bright, weak or strong, good or bad.

You select the colors of your emotions, discordant or harmonious, harsh or quiet, weak or strong.

You select the colors of your acts; cold or warm, fearful or daring, small or big.

Through the power of your creative imagination you catch a vision...you dream a dream.

You visualize yourself as the man you want to be.

You see yourself as a triumphant personality striding toward far horizons of constructive accomplishment.

You see yourself as a master servant of the race, ministering to human needs, radiating happiness.

You see yourself as a builder, making a creative contribution to the evolution of modern civilization.

You strive to make the ideal in your mind become the reality on the canvas of Time.

You select and mix the positive colors of heart, mind and spirit into the qualities of effective living: patience, determination, endurance, self-discipline, work, love and faith.

Each moment of your life is a brush stroke in the painting of your growing career.

There are the bold, sweeping strokes of one increasing, dynamic purpose.

There are the lights and shadows that make your life deep and strong.

There are the little touches that add the stamp of character and worth.

The art of achievement is the art of making life—*your life*—a masterpiece.

THE ART OF
Action

Art is expression; it is mind in action.

First the mental image in the mind of Michelangelo. Then action with hammer and chisel and the emergence of the magnificent statue of David.

Religions, philosophies, formulas, projects, blueprints, programs, plans are inert until action infuses them with power.

The greatest truths of God and the mightiest ideas of man remain static and unfruitful when imprisoned in books and chained to pages of paper.

Action releases truth so it can inspire and regenerate; action releases ideas so they can bless and benefit.

Carlyle defined true art as "the God-like rendered visible."

Your own dreams, hopes, aims, purposes mark time until you start them marching.

The work to be done, the goal you seek, will be achieved only when you get off dead center and make a start. Goethe gave us the magic key: "Only *begin* and then the mind grows heated; only *begin* and the task will be completed."

Your ideas and ideals become dynamic when you do something about them, when you express them in everyday action.

Your dreams come true when you *act* to turn them into realities.

"Art," said Tolstoy, "is human activity having as its purpose the transmission to others of the highest and best feelings to which we have risen."

Action sculptures your life; action sculptures the world. You practice the art of action when you act to bring the good into visibility.

THE ART OF
Adventure

A man practices the art of adventure when he heroically faces up to life...When he says, like Frank Crane: "My soul is a Columbus; and not watery wastes, nor glooming mysteries...shall send me back, nor make me cry 'Enough!'"

When he has the daring to open doors to new experiences and to step boldly forth to explore strange horizons.

When he is unafraid of new ideas, new theories and new philosophies.

When he has the curiosity to experiment...to test and try new ways of living and thinking.

When he has the flexibility to adjust and adapt himself to the changing patterns of life.

When he refuses to seek safe places and easy tasks and has, instead, the courage to wrestle with the toughest problems and difficulties.

When he valiantly accepts the challenge of mountain-top tasks and glories in a job well done.

When he has the moral stamina to be steadfast in the support of those men in whom he has faith and those causes in which he believes.

When he breaks the chain of routine and renews his life through reading new books, traveling to new places, making new friends, taking up new hobbies and adopting new viewpoints.

When he considers life a constant quest for the noblest and best.

When he has the nerve to move out of life's shallows and venture forth into the deep.

When he recognizes that the only ceiling life has is the one he gives it and comes to realize that he is surrounded by infinite possibilities for growth and achievement.

When he keeps his heart young and his expectations high and never allows his dreams to die.

When he concludes that a rut is only another name for a grave and that the only way to stay out of ruts is by living adventurously and staying vitally alive every day of his life.

THE ART OF
America

America is a unique way of life symbolic of the creative arts.

America provides the brushes, oils, pigments, and the canvas on which you can paint your life as you want it to be. You choose your own colors, your own form, design and pattern.

America is any tune you want to play with fife and drum, fiddle or horn to establish the beat and rhythm of the upward march to high goals.

America is a book in which you set down your life by the way you live it. You are the principal character. You *live* your own biography. You are free to be hero or villain, great or mediocre.

America is a stage, and the role you play in the drama of life is up to you.

America is a sports arena, and the rules are written so everyone has a chance to win.

America is an engineering achievement, a bridge over which you can cross the chasm of despair.

America is an architecture with which you can build the tower of your dreams.

America is a sculptor's hammer and chisel with which you can fashion yourself into the man you aim to become.

America is an art of living through which you can reach higher, think bigger, grow greater and live deeper than anywhere else on earth.

THE ART OF Awareness

Thoreau wrote: "Only that day dawns to which we are awake." The art of awareness is the art of learning how to wake up to the eternal miracle of life with its limitless possibilities.

It is rising to the challenge of the stirring old hymn: "Awake my soul, stretch every nerve."

It is developing the deep sensitivity through which you may suffer and know tragedy, and die a little, but through which you will also experience the grandeur of human life.

It is following the philosophy of Albert Schweitzer who teaches "reverence for life," from ants to men; it is developing a sense of oneness with all life.

It is identifying yourself with the hopes, dreams, fears and longings of others, that you may understand them and help them.

It is learning to interpret the thoughts, feelings and moods of others through their words, tones, inflections, facial expressions and movements.

It is keeping mentally alert to all that goes on around you; it is being curious, observant, imaginative that you may build an ever increasing fund of knowledge of the universe.

It is striving to stretch the range of eye and ear; it is taking time to look and listen and comprehend.

It is searching for beauty everywhere, in a flower, a mountain, a machine, a sonnet and a symphony.

It is knowing wonder, awe and humility in the face of life's unexplained mysteries.

It is discovering the mystic power of the silence and coming to know the secret inner voice of intuition.

It is avoiding blind spots in considering problems and situations; it is striving "to see life steadily and see it whole."

It is enlarging the scope of your life through the expansion of your personality.

It is through a growing awareness that you stock and enrich your memory...and as a great philosopher has said: "A man thinks with his memory."

THE ART OF
Becoming Rich

The art of becoming rich is simply to live richly in body, mind, heart and spirit.

You become physically rich when you have rich sensations: When your senses are alert and attuned to life so that the very fact of being alive takes on new dimensions and simple experiences have new meaning...the smell of a rose, the stretch of a muscle, the sight of a mountain, the sound of the surf, the taste of strawberries, the touch of clean white sheets...

You become mentally rich when you think rich thoughts: When you immerse your mind in the noble thoughts of men, preserved through the ages in books; when you are curious to learn all you can about the world and its people, the earth beneath your feet and the farthest star in infinite space; when you develop an appreciation of beauty in painting and sculpture, poetry and music; when you expand your mind to encompass great ideas; when you use the magic of your mind to create and to serve...

You become emotionally rich when you have rich feelings: When you know the radiant glow of obeying noble impulses to give and help and inspire; when you experience the bond of warm friendship and deep affection; when you know the joy of hearing a baby laugh; when you are aware of giving and receiving love...

You become spiritually rich when you discover the riches of the kingdom within: When you have a consciousness of the oneness of all life; when you experience kinship with nature; when you are open to the buoyant spiritual lift of being in tune with the Infinite; when you know the power of meditation and prayer.

The best definition of a rich man is a man with a rich self. What a man *is*, not what he has, is the measure of real wealth.

THE ART OF
Being

The art of being is the assumption that you may possess, this very minute, those qualities of spirit and attitude of mind that make for radiant living.

It is a philosophy of *being today*, instead of becoming in a tomorrow that never comes.

It is recognizing that courage, joy, serenity, faith, hope and love are immediately available now, and proceeding to open yourself so these qualities can be expressed through you in everyday living.

It is following the maxim of Shakespeare: "Assume a virtue though you have it not"...knowing that the dynamic power of habit can build it into your character.

It is being great now, being forgiving now, being tolerant now, being happy now, being successful now, instead of postponing positive and constructive living to some vague and indefinite future.

It is knowing that when we move into the future it becomes the *now*, and that now is the appointed time!

It is facing the fact that your biggest task is not to get ahead of others, but to surpass yourself.

It is wasting no time dreaming about the rich life you may live next year, or ten years from now; it is beginning to live at your best right now, today.

It is heeding the wisdom of the ancient Chinese seer who observed: "A journey of a thousand miles begins with a single step," and it is taking that step today.

It is beginning today to be the man you want to be.

It is developing an awareness of the infinite possibilities in each magic moment.

It is enlarging the *now* by pouring into it intense creative energy.

It is immortalizing the present moment that your life may have eternal significance.

It is coming into a full realization that the Master voiced the secret of victorious *being*, when He declared that the Kingdom of God is not afar off, but that it is *within you now!*

THE ART OF
Being Human

B eing just an ordinary human being wandering along the pathway of life, I've evolved this simple philosophy to guide me:

To affirm that I am proud to be a member of the human race; to recognize that, regardless of color, class or creed, man's destiny is my destiny, that only as we learn to live together will we move forward together.

To accept life as it is and go along with it, bravely trying to change what needs to be changed and serenely adapting myself to what cannot be changed.

To realize that no experience in human life is alien to me and my responsibility is to meet whatever happens to me with fortitude and courage.

To admit that, being human, I am bound to make mistakes, but to make as few as possible and to try to avoid making the same mistake twice.

To recognize the frailties and foibles of human nature and to try to be everlastingly patient, forgiving and understanding.

To promptly forget slights and insults and to hope that others will not hold against me the winged arrows that may in anger or irritation escape my lips.

To share my courage and hope with others and keep my fears, heartaches and disappointments to myself.

To go my way quietly and humbly and not worry too much about mysteries I cannot explain. To do my best here and now and let the future take care of itself.

To be grateful for the precious gift of life with its limitless possibilities. To glory in the power of human beings to rise to great heights and to outdo themselves in miraculous works. To find inspiration in the words of Browning: "A man's reach should exceed his grasp or what's a heaven for?"

To understand that the goodness of God can be known only through human goodness; that when I express the highest and best I express God.

To confront the inevitable fact that I share with all human beings a common end: that someday Death, the kind old nurse, will rock us all to sleep, so we should help each other while we can.

To admit that, being human, I often fail to live up to my own philosophy, but to keep trying nevertheless.

THE ART OF
Being Yourself

The art of being yourself at your best is the art of unfolding your personality into the man you want to be. A famous biologist has said that the possibility of even identical twins being wholly alike is one chance to all of the electrons in the world; each man is a unique individual being.

By the grace of God you are what you are; glory in your selfhood, accept yourself and go on from there.

A good place to begin is by having faith in yourself and your destiny. "Trust yourself," wrote Emerson, "every heart vibrates to that iron string."

Champion the right to be yourself; dare to be different and to set your own pattern; live your own life and follow your own star.

Respect yourself; you have the right to be here and you have important work to do.

Don't stand in your own shadow; get your little self out of the way so your big self can stride forward.

Make the most of yourself by fanning the tiny spark of possibility within you into the flame of achievement.

Follow the advice of Socrates: Know Thyself; know your strengths and your weaknesses; your relation to the universe; your potentialities; your spiritual heritage; your aims and purposes; take stock of yourself.

Create the kind of self you will be happy to live with all your life.

Consider the words of the new convert who prayed: "Oh, Lord, help me to reform the world beginning with *me*."

Be gentle with yourself, learn to love yourself, to forgive yourself, for only as we have the right attitude toward our selves can we have the right attitude toward others.

In the relationship of yourself with all the other selves of the world follow the wise axiom of Shakespeare, who wrote: "To thine own self be true, and it must follow, as the night the day, thou canst not then be false to any man."

THE ART OF
Believing

All that I have seen, wrote Emerson, "teaches me to trust the Creator for all I have not seen."

Believing is a daring adventure into the unseen, it is a radiant faith in the unexplored, the undiscovered, the miracles of the future...

There is *magic* in the art of believing!

Believe! Engrave these words of the Master in your memory: "All things are possible to him that believes."

Believe! Believe in the limitless supply of God's goodness. The universe is filled with more wonders than you can imagine.

Believe! Project a mental picture of your goal in life. Believing is a creative force that brings the visible out of the invisible. *You must believe to achieve.*

Believe! An old Latin proverb reads: "Believe that you have it and you have it."

Believe! There is a mental magnet within you that attracts to you what you *are*. Doubt attracts doubt and faith attracts faith. Have faith in others and you will inspire them to have faith in you.

Believe! Ponder the advice of Frank Crane: "You may be deceived if you trust too much, but you will live in torment if you do not trust enough."

Believe! Believe in life's enduring values. Stand up and be counted for the things that count.

Believe! Believe that you are big enough to master any problem; that you can handle life.

Believe! Believe that you can go on growing now and through all eternity. Drive your stake far out in the universe!

Believe! The magic of believing is for *you*. As Alexandre Dumas wrote: "Where is the man who will save us? We want a man! Don't look so far for this man. You have him at hand. This man, it is you, it is I, it is all of us."

Believe!

THE ART OF
Changing Yourself

Life is constantly pounding you from the outside with millions of hammer blows, but you have the last word as to how those blows will change you.

Man alone, of all creatures of earth, can change his own pattern. Man alone is architect of his destiny.

William James declared that the greatest revolution in his generation was the discovery that human beings, by changing the inner attitudes of their minds, can change the outer aspects of their lives.

History and literature are full of examples of the miracle of inner change—Paul on the Damascus Road...Ernest and the Great Stone Face...the hunchback prince, of the Persian story, who became straight and tall by standing each day before a statue of himself made straight...

You cannot climb uphill by thinking downhill thoughts. If your world is gloomy and hopeless, it is because *you* are gloomy and hopeless. *You must change your mind to change your world.*

Change demands self-discipline. Command yourself and make yourself do what needs to be done.

Change requires the substituting of new habits for old. You mold your character and your future by your thoughts and acts.

Change can be advanced by associating with men and women with whom you can walk among the stars. Meet, mingle and make friends with those who have the upward urge.

Change can be inspired by selecting your own spiritual ancestors from among the great of all the ages. You can practice the kindliness of Lincoln, the devotion of Schweitzer, the vision of Franklin...

Change can be achieved by changing your environment. Let go of lower things and reach for the higher. Surround yourself with the best in books, music and art. Listen to the greatest speakers. Hang on the walls of your home portraits of the men you most admire.

Change can be realized through *conscious evolution*. Moment by moment, day by day, concentrate on becoming the man you want to be.

Change can be accomplished most of all through the power of prayer, because with God all things are possible.

THE ART OF
Common Sense

Common sense is a personal compass for guidance around the rocks and shoals of life.

Common sense is not based on theory; it is not a hypothesis. It is life acted out, it is discoveries made in the crucible of existence. It is the tried and tested experiences of mankind.

Common sense sits in judgment on the centuries, on every science, every religion, every art, every government. It is based on what has been proved true, sound and practical.

Common sense is the voice of the ages. It is the distilled essence of what men have learned about life as expressed in the proverbs and maxims of all nations. "That man is happy who lives on his own labor," observed the Egyptian. "Just scale and full measure injure no man," recorded the Chinese. "Examine what is said and not who speaks," said the Arabian. "An idle brain is the devil's workshop," wrote the English...

Common sense is pragmatic. It is what William James called "the cash value of an idea." It is a method that works, a truth that can be applied.

Common sense is the common denominator of intelligence, the key to right answers.

Common sense recognizes the utter senselessness of war, the irrationality of using death, suffering and destruction as a way of settling disputes.

Common sense observes that crime does not pay, that murder will be found out, that the law of compensation works relentlessly and cannot be escaped.

Common sense is the rock on which every enduring institution and organization must be built.

Common sense is the law of God written into the nature of the universe. It is the sum total of the workable findings of man in his long evolution toward the light.

Common sense is dynamic, not static. It changes as time goes on.

The art of common sense is applying the best wisdom we know today based on all our yesterdays.

THE ART OF
Courtesy

~

The art of courtesy is the practice of the Golden Rule in little things.

It is being courteous even to those who are discourteous. It is striving to avoid a reaction of irritation in spite of the most severe provocation. It is remembering that "a soft answer turneth away wrath."

It is coming forward to meet others with warmth, graciousness and a hospitable spirit.

It is using shock-absorber words to smooth the jars and jolts of daily living; words that express kindness, consideration and gratitude.

It is the wisdom to know that we should love before we think and think before we act.

It is putting people at ease, helping them to relax. It is recognizing the worth of the individual, protecting his dignity, inspiring him to think well of himself.

It is the sympathetic ear and the understanding heart.

It is going the second mile to make things pleasant for others.

It is appreciating what others do for us and letting them know it.

It is being big enough to take the blame for our mistakes and being quick to ask forgiveness for our blunders.

It is recognizing the universal power of a smile; for a sincere smile is courtesy in *every language* and puts a glow in the heart everywhere on earth.

It is emphasizing the *gentle* in gentleman.

It is endeavoring to live with some nobility that we may prove that the age of chivalry isn't dead.

It is keeping constantly in mind the words of Emerson: "Life is not so short but that there is always time enough for courtesy."

THE ART OF
Creating Ideas

Ideas are the beginning of all things.

The world we live in today first existed as ideas in the minds of men...bridges, skyscrapers, automobiles, airplanes, religions, philosophies, governments, symphonies, paintings, poems...*everything!*

Man's future is vast because God has given him unlimited power to create ideas. Man's greatest freedom is freedom to think.

Man's mind has immense scope. "The mind," wrote Lewis Mumford, "is a power station, a storage warehouse, a library, a theatre, a museum, a hall of archives, a court of justice, a seat of government."

Ideas make men giants. The art of creating ideas is man's most challenging quest...

First, a man must win the battle against his own inertia. "There is no expedient to which man will not resort to avoid the real labor of thinking," wrote Joshua Reynolds.

Second, he will learn from Edison, who said, "I am more of a sponge than an inventor." He will sponge up all the data and facts about a problem, look at it from every angle, attack it with power and penetration.

Third, he will harness the power of his subconscious mind. When intense concentration on the conscious level fails to reveal the answer, he will relax, play golf, fish, listen to music, or sleep on the problem. He will use what Oliver Wendell Holmes called "the underground workshop of the mind."

Fourth, he will keep alert to the stream of thought continuously flowing through his mind. Like a prospector panning for gold, he will watch for the idea-nuggets that flash in his consciousness.

Fifth, he will evaluate the ideas he receives. He will reject the inferior ones and polish and improve the good ones.

Sixth, he will turn ideas from dreams into realities. He will make them servants of man.

Millions of ideas are awaiting discovery by the minds of men...ideas that will change the world, build the peace, conquer man's common enemies.

Every man can contribute more if he will think more.

THE ART OF
Crisis

*T*he first lesson of History," wrote Emerson, "is the good of evil. Good is a good doctor, but bad is sometimes a better..."

Crisis is creative.

The crisis of the American Revolution created an explosive new idea in government.

The crisis of plagues and epidemics sweeping the world inspired men to create new miracles in medicine.

The crisis of war has spurred men on, not only to create new weapons to destroy, but also to create new methods of saving, preserving and maintaining life and building an enduring peace.

The crisis of adversity has created the resolve and determination to conquer obstacles and has helped to fashion our greatest men.

Out of crises flow new ideas, new approaches, new patterns, new inventions, new discoveries, new leadership...

Crisis is challenge. It can challenge you to create a new life. Out of disappointment and defeat, out of illness and despair you can find victory.

At a time of crisis you face a turning point. You can go either way, up or down, forward or back. Your choice determines your destiny.

Crisis is a test and those who meet it and overcome it become stronger in the process.

Crisis is your chance to meet a problem head-on, wrestle with it and win.

Crisis burns the dross from the gold; crisis refines.

The art of crisis is rising to meet each new crisis with a heroic spirit.

THE ART OF
Decision

Without the power to decide, a man's thoughts and dreams are like vapor blown in the wind. He goes nowhere until he decides where to go.

Life is made up of little and big decisions, and how a man decides determines the direction of his life.

Decision is the spark that ignites action. Until a decision is made nothing happens.

Decision is the courageous facing of issues, knowing that if they are not faced problems will remain forever unanswered.

Decision does not straddle the fence. It takes a firm stand on one side or the other.

Decision can lead to the mountaintop. It can also cause a man to fall to the valley below. But without decision no mountains are climbed.

Decision is often the difference between greatness and mediocrity. In every man's life there comes a time when he must search for a cause, a work, an ideal to which he can give himself. Whether he says "Yes" or "No" to the challenge will determine his future.

Decision is the freeing of one's self from the morass of fear, doubt, anxiety and uncertainty. It is the courage to risk a wrong decision rather than make no decision at all.

Decision is not blind chance. It is focusing the powers of intelligence, meditation and prayer on the thing to be decided.

"We must make no important decision," wrote St. Ignatius Loyola, "without opening our hearts to love."

Decision need not always be made at once. Deciding to delay making a decision is a decision in itself. Many times it is best for one calmly and expectantly to "wait on the Lord" until more light comes.

Decision often concentrates resolve. A man decides on one great cause or mission as the motivation for his life. He says with St. Paul: "This one thing I do!"

Decision awakens the spirit of man. It gives him a goal, a purpose, a reason for being alive. Once a major decision is made, carrying it out becomes a matter of will and courage and dedication. The great decision comes first, the great work follows.

Decide now who and what you will serve. Decision is the first step toward going somewhere.

THE ART OF
Education

Ashley Montagu, the anthropologist, defined education in these words: *"To nourish and cause to grow."*

The art of education is to continue to grow as long as you live.

Grow from what you are into what you desire to be. Live to learn and learn to live.

Grow a larger concept of education. Every moment brings its lesson. Every person is a teacher. Every place is a schoolroom. Your university is the universe.

Grow in all directions. Cultivate the whole man. Develop a desire for goodness, an eagerness for knowledge, a capacity for friendship, an appreciation of beauty, a concern for others...

Grow in your love of learning. "Love is ever the beginning of Knowledge, as fire is of light," wrote Carlyle.

Grow an inquisitive mind. Remember the Chinese proverb: "He who asks a question is a fool for five minutes; he who does not ask a question is a fool forever." You can learn from everyone and everything.

Grow in awareness. Keep the channels of your senses alert to all that goes on outside of you. Keep your mind alert to the stream of thought received within you.

Grow in new directions. Do not stagnate in the backwash of outworn tradition. Respect the past and learn its lessons, then be alive to inquiry and change. Explore new areas and ideas.

Grow in the deeper levels of the human spirit: contemplation, insight, intuition and prayer. "Spirit," wrote Bernard Eugene Meland, "rises out of structures of consciousness that are receptive to the vision of good."

Grow in wisdom and understanding. Remember this secret from that ancient Chinese volume, *The Book of Changes:* "Every human being can draw in the course of his education, from the inexhaustible wellspring of the divine in man's nature."

Grow through all your years. Take inspiration from Michelangelo, who created works of art unequaled by any other man and yet, in his ninetieth year, regretted that he must die just when he was beginning to learn the ABC's of being a sculptor and painter.

Grow! Man is never finished. Man never arrives. Education never stops.

THE ART OF
Empathy

omeone has made the wise observation that a man wrapped up in himself makes a very small package. Such a man is *self-centered*. The dimensions of his life are dwarfed and limited.

The practice of empathy makes a man *other-centered*. Through the power of his creative imagination empathy enables him to project himself into the consciousness of others that he may know how they think and how they feel.

Sympathy merely mirrors another man's trouble; empathy discovers the causes of the trouble with the searchlight of insight.

Through empathy a man comes to appreciate another person's feelings without becoming so emotionally involved that his judgment is affected.

Through empathy a man learns not to judge others in terms of his own personal interests, likes and dislikes, but in terms of what life means to *them*.

The Sioux Indians expressed the attitude of empathy when they prayed, "Great Spirit, help us never to judge another until we have walked for two weeks in his moccasins."

Through empathy a man may closely identify himself with anyone he may wish to understand. He may seek inspiration from the gifted, the victorious, the happy. He may develop a deep comprehension of the problems of the blind, the crippled, the sorrowing and the defeated.

Through empathy a man may become all men under all conditions of stress and difficulty.

Empathy is the key to leadership. It unlocks the dreams in the hearts of men so the leader can help to make those dreams come true.

Empathy helps to create harmony in the home. Family members may play the roles of each other. For instance, the father can play the part of the son and the son the part of the father, that each may learn to know and appreciate the feelings of the other.

Practicing the art of empathy will enlarge a man's life.

It will broaden his humanity, expand his understanding and inspire tolerance and forbearance, compassion and forgiveness.

THE ART OF
Failure

He who hopes to avoid all failure and misfortune is trying to live in a fairyland; the wise man realistically accepts failures as a part of life and builds a philosophy to meet them and make the most of them.

He lives on the principle of "nothing attempted, nothing gained" and is resolved that if he fails he is going to fail while trying to succeed.

He does not set for himself the impossible ideal of always being successful in everything.

He does the best he can and then with a serene spirit accepts what comes.

He learns from the scientist who said, "At best, research is about 99 percent failure and 1 percent success and the 1 percent is the only thing that counts."

He finds courage in the pages of biography which indicate that our greatest men failed many times. For instance, Louis Pasteur was described as "a scientific Phoenix who arose triumphant from the ashes of his own mistakes."

He recognizes that although he cannot always control what happens to him, he can always control how he responds to his failures.

He observes that the only water that can sink a ship is water that gets inside of it and so he strives to keep all thoughts of failure out of his mind.

He knows that as long as a man keeps his faith in God and in himself nothing can permanently defeat him.

He knows that when the blows of life knock a man down, the important thing is not to stay down. He develops the quality of bounce, rebounding from defeat as a rubber ball rebounds when you throw it to the floor.

He knows that life has its rhythms, as the ebb and flow of the tide, so he learns "to labor and to wait," giving time a chance to work its miracles.

He uses the lessons of failure to build for the future; his mistakes become red stoplights warning him away from highways that lead to defeat.

He learns to fall forward like a good ball carrier in football...to make the most of every failure.

He rises to the challenge of failure as did Mark Twain when he wrote, "A few fly bites cannot stop a spirited horse."

He keeps on going.

He adopts as his talisman the magic words of the ancient seer: "This, too, shall pass away."

THE ART OF

Forgiveness

The art of forgiveness begins when you forgive someone.

It is having a humble spirit and being done with pride and self-pity. It is taking a step toward the practice of forgiveness. Hate is death, forgiveness is life.

Forgiveness works the miracle of change. When Lincoln was asked why he did not destroy his enemies he replied: "If I make my enemies my friends, don't I then destroy them?" When you forgive you change others and you change yourself. You change discord to harmony.

Forgiveness should span the years. You should first forgive yourself for the wrongs you've done to yourself and others, for the mistakes you've made. Then you should forgive and bless all those who have wronged you during your lifetime. Thus you release others and you release yourself. You break the chains of regret and remorse that bind you. You free your mind from the burdens of the past so you may walk victoriously into the future.

Forgiveness works two ways. You must forgive to be forgiven. "He who cannot forgive others," wrote Edward Herbert, "breaks the bridge over which he himself must pass; for every man has the need to be forgiven."

Forgiveness should become a habit. When the Master was asked how often we should forgive, he answered: "Until seventy times seven." He who forgives to infinity will never hate.

Forgiveness should start now. Putting off forgiving only deepens the wound. Clinging to bitterness postpones happiness. Life is short, time is fleeting. Today is the day to forgive.

Forgiveness is the way to personal peace. It is performing mental surgery in yourself, probing deep within to remove hurts, grudges and resentments. It is forgetting wrongs as though they had never been. It is flooding your mind with the powerful medicine of forgiveness that cleanses and heals. It is discovering a serenity you've never known before.

THE ART OF
Freedom

*F*reedom is a *personal thing*.

Freedom is an *open door*, but you must walk through it.

Freedom is a *ladder*, but you must climb it.

Freedom doesn't mean you can do what you please, but it does mean that there isn't anything holding you back from striving to make your finest dreams come true.

Freedom is yours now, this very minute, and what you do with it is up to you. You can aim at the highest goal.

Freedom is an invitation to be creative—to paint, sing, carve, write, build, according to your heart's desire.

Freedom is the opportunity to dedicate your life to the service of others. You can follow your gleam wherever it leads.

Freedom is your right to be yourself, to make mistakes, to fail and try again. No failure is final; freedom always gives you another chance.

Freedom is a blessing to be shared. The fruits of freedom depend upon the interaction of the thoughts, ideas and ideals of men.

Freedom is a wide horizon gleaming with promise. The only chains and shackles you must break are within you. You practice the art of freedom when you make the most of all that freedom offers.

Freedom is God's gift to you. "Where the spirit of the Lord is, there is liberty," wrote Saint Paul.

Thank God for your freedom. It is your key to an inspiring future.

THE ART OF
Friendship

The first step in the art of friendship is to be a friend; then making friends takes care of itself. To be a friend a man should start by being a friend to himself, by being true to his highest and best and by aligning himself with the enduring values of human life that make for growth and progress.

To be a friend a man should strive to be "like the shadow of a great rock in a weary land," to be a source of refuge and strength to those who walk in darkness.

To be a friend a man should believe in the inherent goodness of men and in their potential greatness; he should treat men in a big spirit, expectant of a noble response.

To be a friend a man should strive to lift people up, not cast them down; to encourage, not discourage; to set an example that will be an inspiration to others.

To be a friend a man should be sensitively responsive to the dreams and aims of others and should show sincere appreciation for the contributions others make to the enrichment of his life.

To be a friend a man should practice the companionship of silence and the magic of words that his speech may build and not destroy, help and not hinder.

To be a friend a man should close his eyes to the faults of others and open them to his own.

To be a friend a man should not attempt to reform or reprimand, but should strive only to make others happy if he can.

To be a friend a man should be himself, he should be done with hypocrisy, artificiality and pretense, he should meet and mingle with people in quiet simplicity and humility.

To be a friend a man should be tolerant, he should have an understanding heart and a forgiving nature, knowing that all men stumble now and then, and that he who never made a mistake never accomplished anything.

To be a friend a man should join hands with all people who are working for great principles, great purposes and great causes; he should put his shoulder to the wheel to help achieve common goals.

To be a friend a man should go more than halfway with his fellow men; he should greet others first and not wait to be greeted; he should radiate a spirit of overflowing good will.

To be a friend a man should remember that we are human magnets; that like attracts like, and that what we give we get.

To be a friend a man should recognize that no man knows all the answers, and that he should add each day to his knowledge of how to live the friendly way.

THE ART OF

Getting Along

Sooner or later a man, if he is wise, discovers that life is a mixture of good days and bad, victory and defeat, give and take.

He learns that a man's size is often measured by the size of the thing it takes to get his goat...that the conquest of petty irritations is vital to success.

He learns that he who loses his temper usually loses.

He learns that carrying a chip on his shoulder is the quickest way to get into a fight.

He learns that buck-passing acts as a boomerang.

He learns that carrying tales and gossip about others is the easiest way to become unpopular.

He learns that everyone is human and that he can help to make the day happier for others by smiling and saying, "Good morning!"

He learns that giving others a mental lift by showing appreciation and praise is the best way to lift his own spirits.

He learns that the world will not end when he fails or makes an error; that there is always another day and another chance.

He learns that listening is frequently more important than talking, and that he can make a friend by letting the other fellow tell *his* troubles.

He learns that all men have burnt toast for breakfast now and then and that he shouldn't let their grumbling get him down.

He learns that people are not any more difficult to get along with in one place than another and that "getting along" depends about ninety-eight percent on his own behavior.

THE ART OF
Giving

*I*n gratitude for God's gift of life to us we should share that gift with others. The art of giving encompasses many areas. It is an outgoing, overflowing way of life.

Basically we give what we are. "The thoughts you think," wrote Maeterlinck, "will irradiate you as though you are a transparent vase."

The gifts of *things* are never as precious as the gifts of *thought*.

Emerson said it well: "Rings and jewels are not gifts, but apologies for gifts. The only true gift is a portion of thyself."

We give ourselves when we give gifts of the heart: love, kindness, joy, understanding, sympathy, tolerance, forgiveness...

We give of ourselves when we give gifts of the mind: ideas, dreams, purposes, ideals, principles, plans, inventions, projects, poetry...

We give of ourselves when we give gifts of the spirit: prayer, vision, beauty, aspiration, peace, faith...

We give of ourselves when we give the gift of time; when we are minute builders of more abundant living for others...

We give of ourselves when we give the gift of words: encouragement, inspiration, guidance...

We should give of ourselves with the radiant warmth of sunshine and the glow of the open fire.

We should give our community a good man.

We should give our home a devoted husband and father.

We should give our country a loyal citizen.

We should give our world a lift toward "that one far-off divine event toward which all creation moves."

The finest gift a man can give to his age and time is the gift of a constructive and creative life.

THE ART OF
Good Citizenship

ood citizenship is a personal thing. The good citizen reaches out to others with an open hand, an open mind and an open heart. He sees the potential bigness in the little people. He lifts people up instead of letting them down.

Good citizenship calls for action. The good citizen gets off the sidelines and takes part in the struggle. He recognizes that humanity moves forward not only from the mighty shoves of its great leaders but also from the tiny pushes of the rank and file of the people. He uses the humble ounces of his weight to help tip the scale for what he thinks is right.

Good citizenship applies the power of the ballot. The good citizen uses his vote as a flaming sword to crusade for the kind of city, state, nation and world in which he wants to live.

Good citizenship begins at home. The good citizen observes the law. He helps to keep his city clean. He keeps his house painted, his lawn trimmed and flowers growing in his garden. He champions worthy causes and helps the unfortunate. He strives to be a good neighbor and to do well the thousand and one little things that add up to the big things we all want.

Good citizenship calls for balanced living in the vital areas of work, play, love and worship. The good citizen strives to do his daily work well and thus contribute to human happiness. He takes time to play and to laugh and to look up at the stars. He makes his home and family the center of his activities and takes pride in being a good parent. He leaves room for the life of the spirit.

Good citizenship is built on faith. The good citizen has the daring of a great faith. He lifts his sights above doubt and fear. He believes in the possibilities of world peace and in a growing understanding and cooperation between men. He thinks, talks and lives in harmony with his faith.

The good citizen clings to his great expectation. Though defeat may come and dark clouds appear, he maintains a vibrant faith in the future of mankind.

THE ART OF
Great Life

Great men are little men expanded. Great lives are ordinary lives intensified. *All lives are potentially great.*

The art of great life is marked by emphasis on qualities like these...

It is great to love life. Accept life as a precious gift from the hand of God and strive to make the most of it.

It is great to serve life. The most important thing in life is not what people can do for you but what you can do for people. Lose yourself in a cause bigger than yourself.

It is great to be alive to the best in life. To be alive only to material possessions and goals is to live in the shallows. Launch out into the deep where the treasures are!

It is great to stand for something. Men of principle are the principal men. Character is the bedrock of true greatness.

It is great to seek excellence. Aspire to excel in your chosen work. Adopt the creed of the maker of the immortal Stradivarius violins: "Perfection consists not in doing extraordinary things but in doing ordinary things extraordinarily well."

It is great to have a free mind. Break down the walls of prejudice, fear and limitation. Have the courage to think your own thoughts, speak your own mind and live your own life.

It is great to be gentle. The Chinese philosopher Lao-tze listed gentleness as the first quality of greatness. In an age of push use the magnetic pull of gentleness.

It is great to have creative zest. Have a sense of wonder and curiosity about the world. Have the boundless energy to explore, adventure and experiment with new ideas.

It is great to have great aims. Follow the counsel of Daniel Burnham: "Make no little plans; they have no power to stir men's blood. Make big plans, aim high in hope and work, remembering that a noble, logical diagram, once recorded, will never die."

It is great to keep open to the power of the Infinite. As a huge dam converts the power of a mighty river to create electricity and put it to work, so you can convert the golden river of God's goodness into *spiritual electricity* to help light the world.

It is great to multiply greatness. Feed other minds and help them grow. Guide them in the art of discovery. Inspire others to live great lives.

THE ART OF Happiness

You can't pursue happiness and catch it. Happiness comes upon you unawares while you are helping others. The philosophy of happiness is pointedly expressed in the old Hindu proverb, which reads: "Help thy brother's boat across, and lo! thine own has reached the shore."

Happiness is like perfume—you can't spray it on others without getting some on yourself.

Happiness does not depend upon a full pocketbook, but upon a mind full of rich thoughts and a heart full of rich emotions.

Happiness does not depend upon what happens outside of you but on what happens inside of you; it is measured by the spirit in which you meet the problems of life.

Happiness is a state of mind. Lincoln once said: "We are as happy as we make up our minds to be."

Happiness doesn't come from doing what we like to do but from liking what we have to do.

Happiness comes from putting our hearts in our work and doing it with joy and enthusiasm.

Happiness does not come from doing easy work but from the afterglow of satisfaction that comes after the achievement of a difficult task that demanded our best.

Happiness grows out of harmonious relationships with others, based on attitudes of good will, tolerance, understanding and love.

Happiness is found in little things: a baby's smile, a letter from a friend, the song of a bird, a light in the window.

Happiness comes from keeping constructively busy; creative hobbies are the keys to happy leisure hours and retirement years.

The master secret of happiness is to meet the challenge of each new day with the serene faith that: "All things work together for good to them that love God."

THE ART OF

Hope

The well-known maxim, "While there is life there is hope," has deeper meaning in reverse: *"While there is hope there is life."*

Hope comes first, life follows. Hope gives power to life. Hope rouses life to continue, to expand, to grow, to reach out, to go on.

Hope sees a light where there isn't any. Hope lights candles in millions of despairing hearts.

Hope is the miracle medicine of the mind. It inspires the will to live. Hope is the physician's strongest ally.

Hope is man's shield and buckler against defeat. "Hope," wrote Alexander Pope, "springs eternal in the human breast." And as long as it does man will triumph and move forward.

Hope never sounds retreat. Hope keeps the banners flying.

Hope revives ideals, renews dreams, revitalizes visions.

Hope scales the peak, wrestles with the impossible, achieves the highest aim.

Hope discovered America. In the face of unknown seas and the terror of a mutinous crew, Columbus gave the command of hope: "Sail on! Sail on and on!"

Hope, alone, remained in Pandora's box after all other blessings had escaped. Greek mythology thus proclaims hope as the indispensable blessing of life.

"The word which God has written on the brow of every man," wrote Victor Hugo, "is Hope."

As long as a man has hope no situation is hopeless.

When you reach the end of your rope, use hope to tie a knot in it—and hang on!

THE ART OF
Humility

*T*he art of humility begins with a recognition of our dependence on others and an appreciation of God's gift of life.

A man becomes humble when he sees himself in imagination standing naked, helpless and alone at the dawn of man's creation.

When he realizes that millions of men, in thousands of battles, have given their lives to make him free.

When he is aware of the enormous debt he owes to others who have labored through the ages to fashion the world he lives in. When he acknowledges that he is the heir of infinite riches he did not create.

When he considers how little he knows of all there is to know. When he understands how the philosopher Will Durant felt, when he wrote on his seventy-fifth birthday: "I feel like a drop of water trying to understand the ocean."

When he stands under the stars at night and meditates on his insignificance compared with the vast reaches of the universe.

When he measures his inadequacy in the face of the multitude of undone tasks that face mankind.

When he ponders the miracle of his own body, which, without his conscious thought, controls heartbeat and respiration, digests food, compounds chemicals, renews cells, combats disease, heals wounds, maintaining the equilibrium of his intricate physical being.

Out of such contemplation a man becomes truly humble.

Because he knows so little about so much he becomes teachable, open-minded and flexible. He never stops growing.

Because he realizes his own limitations he becomes more tolerant and understanding of others.

Because he is grateful for the immeasurable contributions others have made to his life he is not blinded by arrogance and pride. He has greater vision because his ego does not get in his way.

He discovers that those of a gentle spirit *do* have the earth for their possession; that humility opens the gates of the mind and heart so greatness can flow through.

THE ART OF
Imagination

"Imagination," said Einstein, "is more powerful than knowledge."

Imagination enlarges vision, stretches the mind, challenges the impossible. Without imagination, thought comes to a halt!

You awaken your imagination through the driving power of *curiosity* and *discontent*.

You *light up* your imagination by stoking your mental fires through the senses—eyes, ears, nose, muscles, skin. You spur your imagination by giving it abundant data with which to work.

You take time for dreams and fantasy, knowing that only as you become as open and receptive as a little child, shall you enter the Kingdom of Ideas.

You rub shoulders with men, watching for the creative sparks that generate new concepts and approaches.

You learn from that great master of imagination Thomas Alva Edison, who when asked the secret of his inventive genius replied, "I listen from within."

You use your imagination to look at everything with fresh eyes, as though you had just come forth from a dark tunnel into the light of day.

Your imagination becomes for you a magic lamp with which to explore the darkness of the unknown that you may chart new paths to old goals.

You recognize the reality of facts, but you use your imagination to penetrate beneath them and to project your thought beyond them in your search for creative answers to problems.

Imagination "stirs up the gift of God in thee." Through your imagination you touch and express the inspiration of the Infinite.

Imagination, in the words of Shakespeare, "gives to airy nothing a local habitation and a name." You reach into the heavens to grasp an idea, then you bring it down to earth and make it work.

THE ART OF

Joy

The art of joy is having a love affair with life.

It is embracing life, drawing close to you all the beauty and wonder and goodness of the universe.

It is having a heart aglow with warmth for all your companions on the journey of life.

It is an expression of inner music. It is radiating joy as does a band of musicians marching down the street.

It is a blend of laughter and tears. Often it is the deep joy that comes to you through the mist of the years as you recall tender memories of joyous days gone by.

It is sharing your joy. "Some people," wrote the poet Walt Whitman, "are so much sunshine to the square inch." The joyous person seems to be plugged in to the sun itself.

It is celebrating life. The Master turned water into wine that the joyous wedding feast might continue. "Be of good cheer," He said. He proclaimed the purpose of his message to men in these words: "That my joy might remain in you and that your joy might be full."

It is the putting forth of all your powers. It is the floodtide of inspiration, the glory of creation. As you work with joy you find joy in your work.

It is looking for the joys that come in small, precious packages and making the most of them, knowing that big packages of joy are few and far between.

It is making the most of now, enjoying what is at hand. It is taking time to enjoy life as you go along.

It is an awareness of the heaven that exists all about you. As Solomon said: "He that hath a bountiful eye shall be blessed." It is making each day your most wonderful day.

Joy is the flag you fly when the Prince of Peace is in residence within your heart.

Joy is love bubbling forth into life.

THE ART OF
Keeping Christmas

How can we best keep Christmas? How can we best defeat the little bit of Scrooge in all of us and experience the glory of the Great Day?

By sinking the shafts of our spirits deep beneath the sparkling tinsel of the surface of Christmas and renewing within us the radiance of the inner meaning of the season.

By following the Star on an inward journey to Bethlehem to stand again in awe and wonder before the Babe in a Manger.

By rediscovering the faith and simplicity of a little child, for of such is the Kingdom of Heaven.

By being still and listening to the angels sing within our hearts.

By quietly evaluating our lives according to the Master's standards as set forth in the Sermon on the Mount.

By reaffirming the supremacy of the spirit in man's conquest of himself.

By rededicating ourselves to the Master's ideals of Peace, Brotherhood and Good Will.

By resolving to *give ourselves away* to others in love, joy and devotion.

By using the light of Christmas to guide us through the darkness of the coming year, refusing to go back to the dim kerosene lamps of the spirit when the brilliant electricity of Christmas is available to show us the way.

THE ART OF
Laughter

Meet the challenge of life with the art of laughter...Take a tip from Will Rogers who observed people with laughter in his eyes and love in his heart and declared: "I never met a man I didn't like."

Learn laughter from little children by thinking their thoughts, dreaming their dreams and playing their games.

Develop a playful attitude toward problems; toss them around; handle them with a light touch.

Practice the advice of the psychiatrist who gives his normal patients this prescription: "Don't take yourself so damned seriously."

Use laughter as a safety valve to keep yourself sane and relaxed. Emerson said it well: "The perception of the Comic is a tie of sympathy with other men, a pledge of sanity. We must learn by laughter as well as by tears and terror."

Remember the old proverb: "A little nonsense now and then is relished by the wisest men."

Consider the power of laughter to prick the balloons of pretense and to deflate stuffed shirts.

Inject laughter into tense situations to save the day; laughter calms tempers and soothes jangled nerves.

Use laughter to set healing vibrations into motion—to fill a room with the sunshine of good cheer.

Guard yourself against the gloomy outlook by recalling the wise statement of Henry Ward Beecher: "A man without mirth is like a wagon without springs...he is jolted disagreeably by every pebble in the road."

Tell the funny side of your difficulties; impersonal contemplation is the secret of laughter and perspective.

Most of all, learn to laugh at yourself; meet each day with a sense of humor.

Laughter is the best medicine for a long and happy life. He who laughs...lasts!

THE ART OF
Leadership

Simply and plainly defined, a leader is a man who has followers. The leader deserves to have followers. He has earned recognition. Authority alone is no longer enough to command respect.

The leader is a great servant. The Master of Men expressed the ideal of leadership in a democracy when he said, "And whosoever will be chief among you, let him be your servant."

The leader sees things through the eyes of his followers. He puts himself in their shoes and helps them make their dreams come true.

The leader does not say, "Get going!" Instead he says, "Let's go!" and leads the way. He does not walk behind with a whip; he is out in front with a banner.

The leader assumes that his followers are working with him, not for him.

He considers them partners in the work and sees to it that they share in the rewards. He glorifies the team spirit.

The leader duplicates himself in others. He is a man builder. He helps those under him to grow big because he realizes that the more big men an organization has the stronger it will be.

The leader does not hold people down, he lifts them up. He reaches out his hand to help his followers scale the peaks.

The leader has faith in people. He believes in them, trusts them and thus draws out the best in them. He has found that they rise to his high expectations.

The leader uses his heart as well as his head. After he has looked at the facts with his head he lets his heart take a look, too. He is not only a boss—he is a friend.

The leader is a self-starter. He creates plans and sets them in motion. He is both a man of thought and a man of action—both a dreamer and doer.

The leader has a sense of humor. He is not a stuffed shirt. He can laugh at himself. He has a humble spirit.

The leader can be led. He is not interested in having his own way, but in finding the best way. He has an open mind.

The leader keeps his eyes on high goals. He strives to make the efforts of his followers and himself contribute to the enrichment of personality, the achievement of more abundant living for all and the improvement of civilization.

THE ART OF
Listening

The key to the art of listening is *selectivity*. You stand guard at the ear-gateway to your mind, heart and spirit. You decide what you will accept...

Listen to the good. Tune your ears to love, hope and courage. Tune out gossip, fear and resentment.

Listen to the beautiful. Relax to the music of the masters; listen to the symphony of nature—hum of the wind in the treetops, bird songs, thundering surf.

Listen with your *eyes*. Imaginatively listen to the sounds in a poem, a novel, a picture.

Listen critically. Mentally challenge assertions, ideas, philosophies. Seek the truth with an open mind.

Listen with patience. Do not hurry the other person. Show him the courtesy of listening to what he has to say, no matter how much you may disagree. You may learn something.

Listen with your heart. Practice empathy when you listen; put yourself in the other person's place and try to hear his problems in your heart.

Listen for growth. Be an inquisitive listener. Ask questions. Everyone has something to say which will help you to grow.

Listen creatively. Listen carefully for ideas or the germs of ideas. Listen for hints or clues which will spark creative projects.

Listen to yourself. Listen to your deepest yearnings, your highest aspirations, your noblest impulses. Listen to the better man within you.

Listen with depth. Be still and meditate. Listen with the ear of intuition for the inspiration of the Infinite.

THE ART OF
Living Each Day

Each day is a lifetime in miniature.

To awaken each morning is to be born again, to fall asleep at night is to die to the day.

In between waking and sleeping are the golden hours of the day.

What we cannot do for a lifetime we can do for a *day-time*.

"Anyone," wrote Robert Louis Stevenson, "can live sweetly, patiently, lovingly, purely, till the sun goes down."

Anyone can hold his temper for a day and guard the words he speaks.

Anyone can carry his burden heroically for one day.

Anyone can strive to be happy for a day and to spread happiness around.

Anyone can radiate love for a day.

Anyone can rise above fear for a day and meet each situation with courage.

Anyone can be kind and thoughtful and considerate for a day.

Anyone can endeavor to learn something new each day and mark some growth.

Sir William Osler pointed out that just as ships are kept afloat by airtight compartments, living in daylight compartments will help us avoid wrecking our lives. Osler gives us a magic word with which to fade the day: *Equanimity*.

The supreme art of living is to strive to live each day well.

When we fail and fall short, let us forgive ourselves and consider the words of Emerson: "Finish every day and be done with it. You have done what you could; some blunders and absurdities have crept in; forget them as soon as you can. Tomorrow is a new day; you will begin it well and serenely and with too high a spirit to be cumbered by your old nonsense."

Live a day at a time and remember that tomorrow is another *today*.

THE ART OF
Living Forever

No man stands alone. Through all the centuries of recorded time, men have set into motion influences that affect your life today...

You are the heir of the ages. Men reaching for the stars have created for you a world of wonder and challenge...

Living in you now are the ideals of the ragged soldiers of Valley Forge, the gallant Pilgrims, the daring explorers and pioneers, the fighters for freedom through all history...

On a more intimate note, your mother, father, teacher, clergyman, friend have their influences into your character...

More enduring than skyscrapers, bridges, cathedrals, and other material symbols of man's achievement are the invisible monuments of wisdom, inspiration and example erected in the hearts and minds of men...

Example has immortal momentum. It has been truly said that a boy does not have to be shown a mark on the wall to measure up to, when there is a man around about the size he wants to be...

Mentor Graham, teacher of Lincoln, is forgotten, but his influence lives forever in the Man for the Ages...

Ideas move through time and space changing the world, making all things new, from the discovery of fire and the invention of the wheel to the development of atomic power...

Words are charged with everlasting power. The radiant words of the Sermon on the Mount light the spirits of each generation. The axioms of the great inspire men to "rise on steppingstones of their dead selves to higher things." Simple words expressing courage, faith and love have immortal significance in the lives of millions...

Your example, your words, your ideas, your ideals can also be projected into the future to live forever in the lives of others...

As you help men grow, as you work for peace, understanding and good will, your influence will merge, with the good influences of men of every age, into the eternal golden stream of God's goodness...

As you throw the weight of your influence on the side of the good, the true and the beautiful, your life will achieve an endless splendor. It will go on in others, bigger, finer, nobler than you ever dared to be.

THE ART OF
Loafing

I loaf and invite my soul," sang the poet Walt Whitman.

The art of loafing is following the philosophy of the vagabond who said, "I turn my back to the wind." It is drifting and dreaming and opening yourself to the inflow of peace and tranquillity.

It is easing the pounding of your heart by the quieting of your mind.

It is relaxing the tension of your body with the music of the singing streams that live in your memory.

It is reminding yourself of the fable of the Hare and the Tortoise that you may know that the race is not always to the swift, that there is more to life than increasing its speed.

It is slowing down to look at a flower, to chat with a friend, to pat a dog, to read a few lines from a book.

It is using your hands to plane a board, paint a picture or plant a garden. It is experiencing the adventure of a change of pace.

It is loafing with one eye open for the flashes of light that may illuminate your mind with the answers you seek.

It is sinking the shafts of your thoughts deep into the eternal well of God's wisdom. It is listening within to the truth that makes men free.

When problems arise, when pressures mount, follow the wise rule Admiral Byrd used when his ship was locked in the ice of the Antarctic: "Give wind and tide a chance to change."

Pause and still your mind. Go to the window and look up at the stars.

The art of loafing can add dimension and scope to your life. It can change your perspective and renew your spirit. Just as rests and pauses are a part of great music, so are they also a part of *great living*.

He who finds time to loaf is a wise man.

THE ART OF

Love

The spectrum of love merges and focuses all of the arts of living.

Friendship, awareness, happiness, *all of the arts of the good life,* are brilliant beads strung on the golden cord of love.

Love is the foundation and the apex of the pyramid of our existence.

Love is the "affirmative of affirmatives"; it enlarges the vision, expands the heart.

Love is the dynamic motivation behind every worthy purpose; it is the upward thrust that lifts men to the heights.

Love is the creative fire, the inspiration that keeps the torch of progress aflame.

Love penetrates the mysteries of life. "Anything," said George Washington Carver, "will give up its secrets if you love it enough."

Love is the dove of peace, the spirit of brotherhood; it is tenderness and compassion, forgiveness and tolerance.

Love is the supreme good; it is the overflowing life, the giving of ourselves to noble ends and causes.

Love is down to earth and it reaches to the highest star; it is the valley of humility and the mountaintop of ecstasy.

Love is the spiritual magnetism that draws men together for the working of miracles. "Ten men banded together in love," wrote Carlyle, "can do what ten thousand separately would fail in."

Love is the perfect antidote that floods the mind to wash away hatred, jealousy, resentment, anxiety and fear.

Love alone can release the power of the atom so it will work for man and not against him.

Love, in the words of the Master, is the shining commandment: LOVE ONE ANOTHER.

The art of love is God at work through you.

THE ART OF *Marriage*

*H*appiness in marriage is not something that just happens. A good marriage must be created. In the art of marriage the *little things* are the *big things*...

It is never being too old to hold hands.

It is remembering to say, "I love you," at least once each day.

It is never going to sleep angry.

It is at no time taking the other for granted; the courtship shouldn't end with the honeymoon, it should continue through all the years.

It is having a mutual sense of values and common objectives; it is standing together facing the world.

It is forming a circle of love that gathers in the whole family.

It is doing things for each other, not in the attitude of duty or sacrifice, but in the spirit of joy.

It is speaking words of appreciation and demonstrating gratitude in thoughtful ways.

It is not expecting the husband to wear a halo or the wife to have the wings of an angel. It is not looking for perfection in each other. It is cultivating flexibility, patience, understanding and a sense of humor.

It is having the capacity to forgive and forget.

It is giving each other an atmosphere in which each can grow.

It is finding the room for the things of the spirit. It is a common search for the good and the beautiful.

It is establishing a relationship as counseled by Louis K. Anspacher, in which "the independence is equal, the dependence is mutual and the obligation is reciprocal."

It is not only marrying the right partner, it is *being* the right partner.

It is discovering what marriage can be, at its best, as expressed in the words Mark Twain used in a tribute to his wife: "Wherever she was, there was Eden."

THE ART OF
Mastering Fear

Fear is a wild horse that needs a tight rein, for it is both friend and foe, both good and evil, and to live effectively a man must learn to master it...

By utilizing the intuitive warning system of fear as a shield against real danger.

By harnessing the energizing power of fear for flight or fight when an emergency strikes.

By using the fear of insecurity, defeat and failure as a lash and spur to high achievement.

By guarding against fear's power to destroy through recalling the ancient legend of the Plague that went to Bagdad to kill five thousand people. Fifty thousand died instead and when the Plague was questioned, it replied: "I killed five thousand as I said I would, the others died of fright!"

By flooding the dark corners of fear and superstition with the bright light of reason and knowledge, thus mapping the unknown, overcoming fancy with fact, dispersing hobgoblins of the imagination and revealing the truth that sets men free.

By accepting the fact that old age and death are natural and inevitable, that to fear them is futile, and that they can best be faced with a calm and quiet mind by ignoring them and gallantly living a day at a time.

By finding inspiration in the words of Cardinal Newman: "Fear not that your life shall come to an end but rather that it shall never have a beginning."

By willingly taking the risk of enriching adventures tinged with danger, knowing that the sheltered and protected life misses much and that as the Bard of Avon expressed it: "Cowards die many times before their deaths; the valiant never taste of death but once."

By facing fear boldly and practicing the precept of Emerson: "Do the thing you fear and the death of fear is certain."

By coming into alignment with the great spiritual laws of the universe and learning that "God has not given us the spirit of fear, but of power and of love and of a sound mind."

By discovering that the mightiest law of all is this: "Perfect love casts out fear."

By beholding the power of faith to work miracles, as expressed in these inspiring words: "Fear knocked at the door. Faith opened it. And lo, there was no one there!"

THE ART OF
Maturity

he distilled experience of many men has resulted in discoveries like these about the art of mature living...

That life is too short to be wasted in hatred, revenge, faultfinding, prejudice, intolerance and destruction.

That only the affirmative approach inspires progress. We should follow the wise advice of Charles W. Eliot and "cultivate a calm nature, expectant of good."

That our basic direction should always be toward *wholeness* of life. The great life built on deep and enduring values. Like a giant tree, we should grow from within.

That no outstanding work is done alone. Miracles can be achieved when we don't care who gets the credit.

That we should not dodge reality or turn our backs on situations that must be faced. Private bravery is the price of personal victory.

That it is never wise to become too elated or too discouraged. As Robert Louis Stevenson suggested, we should strive to "go on in fortune and misfortune like a clock during a thunderstorm."

That a few troubles and a little pain are good for us and help us to grow. We should not complain that the rosebush has thorns but should rejoice because it bears roses.

That time is the great healer of hurts, sorrows and disappointments. When one door closes another will open if we don't lose heart.

That it is wiser to judge a man by how he lives than by what he says.

That modernization in all things is a good rule. It is wise to live a balanced and varied life without permitting anyone or anything to enslave us.

That we must learn to distinguish between the important and unimportant. Then trifles will not trip us up and we can devote our lives to the meaningful and significant.

That there is no time like the present for putting into effect the seasoned wisdom of our years. It is now or never if we are to avoid an old age of regret and remorse.

That the man who aligns his life with the good and true need fear no evil.

THE ART OF
Memory

Tomorrow's memory depends upon today's impressions. The art of memory is seeking impressions which will enrich your life. It is the art of remembering what will *help* and forgetting what will *hinder*.

Your memory builds your personality, your personality builds your character, and your character determines your destiny.

Memory is an art gallery in which you can collect beauty. You can say with Emerson, "The landscape belongs to me!"—and so it does, no matter who owns the land. Through memory you can possess the world and all its beauty!

Memory is a mental bank account. In it you can deposit the treasure of man's mind so that you can withdraw hope, faith and courage in your time of need. You can be a mental millionaire!

Memory is a record of your personal experience. It is a record of trial and error, defeat and success. Past failures will warn you against repeating them. Past victories will inspire you to set new marks of achievement. Through memory you can focus the things you've learned in the past on the life you are living today.

Memory is your link with the centuries. All that men have remembered and set down in print through the ages is a precious legacy to you. The miracle of memory gives continuity to life.

Memory is a form of immortality. Those you remember never die. They continue to walk and talk with you; their influence is with you always.

Memory is something you create for others. "If you make your children happy now," wrote Kate Douglas Wiggin, "you'll make them happy twenty years from now by the memory of it." The quality of your life will determine the memories others will have of you.

Memory keeps the past alive; and a good past is a bundle of todays well lived.

"Memory," wrote Jean Paul Richter, "is the only paradise from which we cannot be driven."

THE ART OF

Miracles

Out of a block of ivory, Pygmalion chiseled the form of a beautiful woman, Galatea. As he worked with inspired zeal a miracle happened. Galatea came to life!

Many potentially happy and successful people are imprisoned in the ivory of defeat and despair. You can release them to *new* life through the miracle-working power of your inspiring influence.

"One single ray of light," wrote Arnold Bennett, "one single precious hint, will clarify and energize the whole mental life of him who receives it."

Work miracles with praise. Appreciation accelerates accomplishment. Men go on to bigger things when they are made to feel that their work is worthwhile.

Work miracles by painting visions. Help men to see themselves as the men they can become.

Work miracles by having faith in others. Thomas Edison was sent home from school because his teacher said he was hopeless. Years later he wrote: "I won out because my mother never, for a single moment, lost faith in me."

Work miracles by giving courage. Many ideas have failed to be realized because men lacked the courage to see them through. Promising careers have been abandoned because men were afraid. Cheer people on. Instill courage in their hearts.

Work miracles by rousing the imagination. You can never tell what will happen when you set a man's mind on fire with a great dream or purpose. Mentor Graham, Lincoln's teacher, lighted a fire that made a President.

Work miracles by expecting great things. Men will rise to do the seemingly impossible to justify the high expectations you hold for them.

Work miracles by counseling patience. Many a man has turned and left the dock just before his ship came in. Stress the wisdom of working and waiting. Time has great power to solve problems.

Work miracles by setting a good example. Others will catch your spirit! The power of a good example is the greatest miracle-working power of all.

Work with God to inspire men to come alive to their infinite possibilities.

THE ART OF
Parenthood

O f all the commentaries on the Scriptures," wrote John Donne, "good examples are the best."

In practicing the art of parenthood an ounce of example is worth a ton of preachment.

Our children are watching us live, and what we *are* shouts louder than anything we can say.

When we set an example of honesty our children will be honest.

When we encircle them with love they will be loving.

When we practice tolerance they will be tolerant.

When we demonstrate good sportsmanship they will be good sports.

When we meet life with laughter and a twinkle in our eye they will develop a sense of humor.

When we are thankful for life's blessings they will be thankful.

When we express friendliness they will be friendly.

When we speak words of praise they will praise others.

When we confront failure, defeat and misfortune with a gallant spirit they will learn to live bravely.

When our lives affirm our faith in the enduring values of life they will rise above doubt and skepticism.

When we surround them with the love and goodness of God they will discover life's deeper meaning.

When we set an example of heroic living they will be heroes.

Don't just stand there pointing your finger to the heights you want your children to scale. *Start climbing and they will follow!*

THE ART OF
Peace

⌣

"Lord make me an instrument of Thy peace…" Thus begins the inspired prayer of Saint Francis of Assisi. Peace can be achieved only *through people!*

World-wide peace and peace in our little worlds of home, family, office, industry, community…depend upon each one of us putting into action the art of peace…

Peace is God on both sides of the table in a conference.

It is putting the power of good will to work.

It is sanity, maturity and common sense in human relationships.

It is open-mindedness. It is a willingness to listen as well as to speak. It is looking at both sides of a situation objectively.

It is patience. It means keeping our tempers and rising above petty irritations. It is counting to ten and avoiding hasty and impulsive decisions.

It is having the courage and humility to admit mistakes and to take the blame when we are wrong.

It is tact. Tact has been defined as the ability to pull the stinger of a bee without getting stung.

It is vision. It is taking the long look. It is being willing to give up individual advantages for the common good.

It is straight thinking. It is recognizing that iron curtains *are not metal, but mental,* and that they are woven of fear, prejudice and mistrust.

It is a quality of the heart as well as the head. It is a warmth, an enthusiasm, a magnetism that reaches out and draws people together in understanding and love.

It is a mighty faith in the goodness of God and the potential greatness of man.

THE ART OF
Personal Efficiency

To manage others successfully, a man must first manage himself. Personal efficiency is creative self-management. It is not getting ahead of others, but getting ahead of yourself.

It is having the drive to get started on the task at hand. "Life leaps like a geyser," wrote Alexis Carrel, "for those who drill through the rock of inertia."

It is experimenting to find the best, easiest and quickest ways of getting things done.

It is putting first things first, doing one thing at a time and developing the art of intensive concentration.

It is breaking big tasks down into their smaller parts, simplifying the complex, finishing the big job one step at a time.

It is not being a slave to system but making system a slave to you.

It is making notes and letting pencil and paper remember for you.

It is using Kipling's "six honest serving men"—What and Why and When and How and Who and Where.

It is building the efficient mentality of balance, perception, organization, ability and stamina.

It is seeking the counsel of wise men in person and through their writings and using their wisdom and experience to help you to live efficiently.

It is weaving the cables of constructive habit so that right action will become automatic. In sport and in business good habits mark the champion.

It is having a goal and mapping out a personal program of how to reach it.

It is setting up personal incentives—promising yourself rewards for work completed.

It is guiding your life instead of drifting.

It is organizing your personal life for efficient living in all the important areas: work, play, love and worship.

It is making time live for you by making the most of every minute.

THE ART OF
Perspective

*S*aid the Emperor Marcus Aurelius: *"Live as on a mountain."*

Mountain heights cause spirits to soar. How can one be mentally small who associates with the magnificent bigness of mountains?

The mountaintop man lives on an invisible mountain of the mind.

His perspective is broad, his outlook far-reaching.

His spirit towers above the storms of life.

His mind is lifted up, above doubt, cynicism and despair.

His vision is high above the fog of petty things.

He looks beyond the obstacles to the promised land of tomorrow.

He sees the rainbows while little men battle with phantom shadows in the valley.

He sees the sun in the east while valley-dwellers burn their tiny lamps in darkness.

His head is in the clouds, but his feet are bedded in the solid rock of Fact and Reason.

He takes the risks; he dares the sky.

He lives with the stars of his ideals, and although he may never grasp them he keeps reaching toward them.

THE ART OF
Power

~~~~~~

*R*eally great men," wrote Ruskin, "have the feeling that the greatness is not in them but *through* them."

You stand at the pinnacle of life, and you can be a channel for mighty streams of power.

The art of power is the opening of yourself to all the sources of power at your command...

The power of wisdom. All the great thoughts of the thinkers of all ages are yours to use. You are the heir of more accumulated knowledge and experience than man has *ever before possessed. You are standing on the shoulders of giants!*

The power of thought. All great living must spring, like a fountain, from within your mind. The quality of the thoughts you think will determine your destiny.

The power of the heart. Emotional drive is the mark of the dynamic achievers. When you put your heart in your work, even so-called impossibilities become possible.

The power of a dream. Great dreams become obsessions which will not be denied. If you are willing to pay the price, you can make your dream come true. "Now and then, not often," wrote Emerson, "a man forgets himself into immortality."

The power of people. Character and ideals are catching. When you associate with men who aspire to the highest and best, you expose yourself to the qualities that make men great.

The power of the spirit. Even Napoleon came to recognize that the spirit is the greatest power of all. After his attempted military conquest of the world had failed he wrote: "There are only two powers in the world, the spirit and the sword. In the long run the sword will always be conquered by the spirit."

The power of the Infinite. Powerful forces come to your aid when you keep in tune with the Infinite. "When we pray," declared the scientist Alexis Carrel, "we link ourselves with the inexhaustible power that spins the universe."

You are a divinely appointed guardian of all the powers man has evolved since time began. It is your duty to use these powers for man's continued growth and development and to pass them on renewed and enlarged to those who will follow you.

THE ART OF
Prayer

*T*he key to the art of prayer is thought. As we think so we pray.

The highest level of prayer is to think God's thoughts after Him, to attune our lives to love, hope, faith, justice, kindness; to become open channels for the goodness of God.

Prayer is quiet meditation about eternal values. It is the mind adventuring in the universe. Prayer moves with the instantaneous speed of thought, through infinite space, to the four corners of the earth, to the depth of the human heart, to the mountaintop of aspiration...

Prayer is a cup held high to be filled. It is an inward quest for inspiration. It is mentally reaching out for the great thoughts and illuminations of man in his continual search for meaning.

Prayer does not change God, it changes us. It deepens insight, increases intuitive perceptions, expands consciousness. It transforms personality.

Prayer opens doors to let in God and let out self, to let in love and let out hate, to let in faith and let out fear.

Prayer helps us to find ourselves. By praying not to get more, but to *be* more, we discover a way to serve, a purpose for which to live, a dream to make real.

Prayer brings God into our relationships with our fellow men. It applies spiritual perspective to the creative solution of human problems. We gain a wider awareness of the needs of others and a wiser knowledge of how to respond.

Prayer helps us to find the way, just as a hunter lost in the woods climbs a tall tree to get his bearings.

Prayer is thinking and thanking. It is thinking of our many blessings and accepting them with a thankful spirit.

Prayer works in the mind as a healing force. It calms the patient, enlightens the physician, guides the surgeon, and it often victoriously applies the power of the spirit when all seems lost. It proves, over and over again, the truth of Tennyson's words: "More things are wrought by prayer than this world dreams of."

Prayer puts us on God's side. It aligns us with life's highest purposes, aims and ideals.

Prayer is power always available. In *The Practice of the Presence of God*, Brother Lawrence said that even amidst the clatter of pots and pans in the monastery kitchen, "I possess God in as great a tranquility as when on my knees."

Prayer is dedicating our thought, feeling and action to the expression of goodness. It is to become like a window through which the light of God shines.

THE ART OF

Progress

The art of progress is the story of man's relentless determination to improve his condition.

Man, genus Homo, held back by tyrants, dark ages, ignorance, fear, economic disaster and war, yet ultimately breaking the shackles and marching forward to the music of his greater destiny.

Caves, sod huts, log cabins, hammers and nails and frame buildings, brick on brick, then steel girders swinging through space and skyscrapers against the skyline.

Rough-hewn wooden wheels, faster-moving wheels of wagons, gasoline buggies, steam engines, modern automobiles and wheels lifted from the earth by the wings of planes.

Strange hieroglyphics carved on the walls of ancient temples, discovery of paper; monks in the monasteries copying the Holy Bible with quill pens; Gutenberg and movable type, and the roar of a million printing presses.

Slavery and serfdom, whipping posts and stocks, then the awakening of the human spirit and the vision of freedom and the brotherhood of man.

Galileo peering into the night sky with an iron pipe for a telescope, and then a giant lens that looks a billion light-years into space.

The Wright brothers, airborne for only ten seconds and one hundred feet on the first flight, and now man in orbit around the earth.

Smoke signals, tapping of a telegraph key, voice over a wire, radio, television and Telstar in the heavens.

Crude, agonizing primitive surgery without anesthesia, and now the magic of deep sleep while miracles are performed.

Columbus crossing the Atlantic in the forty-two-foot ship the *Nina*, Fulton and his steamboat, floating cities plowing the deep, and jet planes making the world a neighborhood.

Candles, oil lamps, Franklin flying his kite into a thunder cloud, and Edison illuminating the world with the first electric light.

Clubs, bows and arrows, fire and catapults, gunpowder, artillery, bombing planes, and then the splitting of the atom making man a titan with the power to destroy civilization or to take a great leap forward in human progress.

Man delayed by ten thousand detours, yet rising after each fall, always building stronger and higher the things he destroys and triumphantly marching forward under the go light of progress, leaving giant footprints on the sands of time.

THE ART OF
Reading

To practice the art of reading, develop a hungry, curious, questing mind and then seek your answers in books...You open doors when you open books...doors that swing wide to unlimited horizons of knowledge, wisdom and inspiration that will enlarge the dimensions of your life...

Through books you can live a thousand lives in one. You can discover America with Columbus, stand with Lincoln at Gettysburg, work in the laboratory with Edison and walk the fields with St. Francis...

Through books you can encompass in your imagination the full sweep of world history. You can watch the rise and fall of civilizations, the ebb and flow of mighty battles and the changing pattern of life through the ages...

Through books you can enrich your spirit with the Psalms, the Beatitudes, the thirteenth chapter of First Corinthians and all the other noble writings that are touched with divine fire...

Through books you can know the majesty of great poetry, the wisdom of the philosophers, the findings of the scientists...

Through books you can start today where the great thinkers of yesterday left off, because books have immortalized man's knowledge. Thinkers, dead a thousand years, are as alive in their books today as when they walked the earth.

Through books you can orient your life to the world you live in, for books link the past, the present and the future.

Read, then, from the vast storehouse of books at your command!

Read several books at a time, turning from one to the other as your mood changes...a biography, a novel, a volume of history, a book about your business.

Read with a red pencil in your hand, underlining the important passages, so you can quickly review the heart of the book.

Read something each day. Discipline yourself to a regular schedule of reading. With only fifteen minutes a day you can read twenty books in a year...

Read to increase your knowledge, your background, your awareness, your insight...

Read to lead...read to grow!

THE ART OF
Relaxation

Modern man must learn to break the tensions of daily living or the tensions will break him.

He must learn to bend with the stresses and strains like a tree in the wind. He must develop the resiliency of spirit to spring erect again after the storm has passed.

He first relaxes his mind by thinking thoughts of peace, quietness and tranquility. He mentally pictures the placid pool amidst whispering pines and puts himself in tune with nature's calming mood.

He strives to carry an inner serenity with him so that even amidst a whirl of activity he will not lose his poise. He learns "to cooperate with the inevitable" and he accepts life with faith in the ultimate triumph of right and good.

He relaxes his body by imitating a lazy person—a boy on the beach in the sun—a man in a boat fishing. He takes a tip from the circus clown who says that the way he avoids being injured in his tumbles is by making his body become "like an old rag doll."

He exercises—walks, stretches, works in the garden, plays golf—knowing that physical tiredness invites relaxation and sleep.

He knows that confusion is one of the chief causes of tension so he organizes his work, puts first things first, does one thing at a time, avoids hurry and develops a spaciousness of mind.

He uses the soothing beauty of great music to calm his nerves.

He observes that the face with a frown marks the tense person, and that the face with a smile is a symbol of relaxation, so he strives to meet life with a sense of humor. He learns not to take himself too seriously and to laugh at himself now and then.

He takes time for meditation. He accepts the wise counsel of Emerson, who wrote: "Place yourself in the middle of the stream of power and wisdom which animates all whom it floats, and you are without effort impelled to truth, to right and a perfect contentment."

He recognizes that relaxed living is a way of life and strives to manage body, mind, heart and spirit as efficiently as he manages his business.

THE ART OF
Renewal

*Y*our birthday is the beginning of your own *personal* new year.

Your first birthday was a beginning, and each new birthday is a chance to *begin again*, to start over, to take a new grip on life...

It is time to consider the wisdom of Socrates: "The unexamined life is not worth living." It is a time to re-evaluate your past as a guide to your future.

It is a time to remind yourself that "saints are sinners who keep on trying."

It is a time to toss old hatreds, resentments, grudges and fears into the wastebasket of life; a time to forgive and forget, a time to stretch your soul.

It is a time to list the things you have left undone and to do something about them; the visits you've failed to make, the words unspoken, the letters unwritten, the tasks unfinished.

It is a time to dust off your dreams and shine up your ideals.

It is a time to browse through the precious old books that have meant the most to you that you may rediscover illuminating phrases and sentences to light your pathway into the future.

It is a time to give thanks to God, and to man, for the riches that have been poured into your life; a time to appreciate anew the beauty and wonder of the world.

It is a time to rededicate your life to those things which are enduring, recognizing with William James that "the great use of life is to spend it on something that will outlast it."

It is a time to resolve to *add life to your years*, for as Philip James Bailey points out, "he most lives who thinks most, feels the noblest, acts the best."

THE ART OF

Repainting the Angel

The statuette of an angel holding the hand of a little boy had been placed on a neglected back shelf in an antique shop. It was covered with soot and dust, lost amidst the clutter of jars, dishes and ornaments.

A man browsing through the shop discovered the figurine and took it in his hands. He had an inspiration! He would rescue it from oblivion, restore it, and give it a place of honor among his Christmas decorations.

At home, in his basement workshop, the man covered the angel and the child with glistening white paint. Then he painted the wings of the angel and the hair of the little boy with sparkling gold. Each brush stroke worked magic. The old grime-covered statuette vanished and a shining new one appeared. The statuette was transformed before his eyes into a thing of radiant beauty.

As the man painted, he thought: "Isn't this what happens to people at Christmas? They come to the end of the year dust-covered from the struggle. And then Christmas inspires them to repaint the better angels of their natures with love and joy and peace."

The art of repainting the angel! This is man's lifelong task. Never to stay down in the dust and the dirt. Heroically to rise again after each fall. To create a new life.

Repainting the angel! There is a hidden goodness within every man, and he has the power to bring it forth.

Repainting the angel! A man need never lose his ideals, dreams and purposes. He can always make them gleam again with the glory of renewed hope.

Repainting the angel! A man always has another chance to restore the image of his best self, to regain lost ground, to start over again.

Repainting the angel! Each high thought a man thinks works magic. It helps to transform him and renew his spirit. Just as gold paint will change a statuette, golden thoughts will change a man.

THE ART OF
Retirement

The art of retirement can be summed up briefly in this way: *Don't retire...aspire!*

Retire means to move back, retreat, withdraw.

Aspire means to move forward, to seek the best.

Aspire! Retirement does not mean that you are all through. It means that you have experienced a big *breakthrough* to a new freedom, with the time to do the things you've always wanted to do.

Aspire to make the most of each new day. In the morning think first of the words of the psalmist: "This is the day the Lord hath made, let us rejoice and be glad in it."

Aspire to widen your horizons. See new people and places. Adventure across America and around the world.

Aspire to serve. Work now for those causes you've always believed in. Lend a hand to worthy organizations and movements.

Aspire to grow. Stretch your mind with the thoughts of great thinkers. Live many lives through the pages of biography. Explore the earth and the stars. Now you have time to read!

Aspire to discover the greatness within yourself that you've never had the time to develop before. Paint, carve, play a musical instrument, invent, write a book, plant a garden...*create!*

Aspire to maintain a youthful attitude toward life. Harry Emerson Fosdick said it well: "It is magnificent to grow old if only one stays young."

Aspire to be an inspiration to others. What you are counts more than what you do. Let your light shine. Be a source of strength and courage. Share your wisdom. Radiate love.

Aspire to attain an awareness of the joy of living. Celebrate life! Remember the words of Santayana: "The young man who has not wept is a savage, and the old man who will not laugh is a fool!"

Aspire to realize the power of the spirit. Seek the quietness and solitude for which you have longed. Think and meditate. Be still and know the serenity of inner peace.

Aspire to live all of your life. Rise to the challenge of these words from a letter written by Justice Oliver Wendell Holmes on his ninety-first birthday: "Life seems to me like a Japanese picture which our imagination does not allow to end with the margin. We aim at the infinite and when our arrow falls to earth it is in flames."

Aspire!

THE ART OF
Reverence for Life

*A*lbert Schweitzer's principle legacy to mankind consists of three words, sealed by a life that was a triumphant example of their power.

At sunset one evening, while journeying up the Ogowe River in Africa, Schweitzer's mind lighted up with a phrase which brought his whole philosophy of life into sharp focus: *Reverence for life*.

As a jungle doctor Schweitzer founded a hospital in Africa which grew from a converted chicken coop into a world-famous institution. Here for half a century Schweitzer practiced his philosophy of reverence for life. He was called "a genius of compassion."

"We are like waves that do not move individually but rise and fall in rhythm," wrote the great man. "To share, to rise and fall in rhythm with life around us is a spiritual necessity."

The phrase *Reverence for life* is simple and direct. It was Schweitzer's fervent hope that though he might be forgotten, these words would live. He wanted others to understand them and use them.

We can make these three dynamic words a part of our lives and practice the art of *Reverence for life* in these ways...

By becoming aware that God is the source of all life and that we are one with life. "The good man," said Schweitzer "is the friend of all living things."

By having reverence for ourselves and our own God-given talents and abilities and dedicating them to helping others. By seeking and finding a work through which we can best contribute to the lives of others. Schweitzer often quoted the Master's secret: "He who loses his life shall find it."

By always reaching out to life, to help life to grow, to express itself, and to fulfill its highest destiny.

By striving to live affirmatively. By looking for the good in life and glorifying it.

By having a deep sense of obligation for the precious gift of life. By giving of ourselves that we may repay life, at least in some small measure, for the infinite treasures it pours at our feet.

By coming to know that *Reverence for life* is the very heart of our relations with our fellow men; that we should reverence each other, recognize that we are a part of each other, and live together in a spirit of love.

By realizing that when we war on life we war on ourselves, and that *Reverence for life* is the only pathway to the Kingdom of Peace and Brotherhood.

THE ART OF
Revolution

Revolution is the process of drastic change.

Sometimes there is the need of *personal revolution* within ourselves.

In a personal revolution you are your own enemy and self-conquest is your goal.

A personal revolution is a revolt against wrong, despondent, hopeless thinking.

It is a bold offensive to change habits, thought patterns, actions and establish a new way of life.

It is an about-face. It is turning a corner, taking a new road, moving in a new direction.

It is breaking the bonds of slavery to the past so that you may walk in freedom.

It is implanting creative and constructive thoughts in your mind, to destroy the weeds of negative thinking.

It is sweeping away the decaying foundations of your life that stronger and more enduring ones may be laid for you to build upon.

It is smashing destructive idols and images and gaining a new vision of the person you would become.

It is shaking yourself awake, coming alive, re-establishing your hopes and dreams.

It is waging a battle against complacency, self-satisfaction and inertia. It is stopping drift. It is grabbing the oars and rowing with purpose.

It is overcoming the failure complex by beginning to act as though you cannot fail.

It is a declaration of independence from all that would drag you down, and it is reaching out for all that will lift you up.

It is overthrowing fear and putting faith on the throne.

THE ART OF
Selling

hen everybody sells, goods, services and ideas move faster, and prosperity is achieved.

Selling is not limited to people called salesmen, for we all have something to sell, and that includes *you!*

When everybody sells, we create a mental and emotional climate of friendliness and good will that makes buying a joyous, happy adventure.

Customers are won and held through a multitude of acts and attitudes. Here are some of the things that represent the art of selling at its best:

Courteous words instead of sharp retorts.

Smiles instead of blank looks.

Enthusiasm instead of dullness.

Response instead of indifference.

Warmth instead of coldness.

Understanding instead of the closed mind.

Attention instead of neglect.

Patience instead of irritation.

Sincerity instead of sham.

Consideration instead of annoyance.

Remembering people instead of forgetting them.

Facts instead of arguments.

Creative ideas instead of the humdrum.

Helpfulness instead of hinderance.

Giving instead of getting.

Action instead of delay.

Appreciation instead of apathy.

Everyone selling together blends hearts and minds and spirits, as the musicians in an orchestra harmonize musical tones, to create a mighty symphony of prosperity.

Let's earn more business by deserving the business we have.

Let's roll out the red carpet for the most important person in the world...the customer.

Let's everybody sell!

THE ART OF
Simplicity

"implicity, simplicity, simplicity!" wrote Thoreau. "I say let your affairs be as one, two, three and not as a hundred or a thousand."

The art of simplicity is simply to *simplify...*

Simplicity avoids the superficial, penetrates the complex, goes to the heart of the problem and pinpoints the key factors.

Simplicity does not beat around the bush. It does not take winding detours. It follows a straight line to the objective. Simplicity is the shortest distance between two points.

Simplicity does not elucidate the obscure, it emphasizes the obvious.

Simplicity solves problems. Listen to the testimony of Charles Kettering, a genius of modern research: *"The problem when solved will be simple."*

Simplicity discovers great ideas; a swinging cathedral lamp inspired the pendulum, watching a tea kettle led to the steam engine, a falling apple revealed the law of gravitation.

Simplicity is a mark of greatness. "To be simple is to be great," wrote Emerson. Only little men pretend; big men are genuine and sincere.

Simplicity has given all the big things little names: dawn, day, hope, love, home, peace, life, death.

Simplicity is eloquent: it is the Twenty-third Psalm and the Gettysburg Address.

Simplicity uses little words. It practices the wisdom of Lincoln, who said, "Make it so simple a child will understand; then no one will misunderstand."

Simplicity deepens life. It magnifies the simple virtues on which man's survival depends: humility, faith, courage, serenity, honesty, patience, justice, tolerance, thrift.

Simplicity is the arrow of the spirit!

THE ART OF
Staying Home

A home should be a stockade, a refuge from the flaming arrows of anxiety, tension and worry.

An old art needs to be rediscovered: the art of staying home, the renewing power of love and joy and peace within the home.

Stay home to gather the family together. Let dinnertime be a time of candlelight, music and conversation, serious and gay. Share a great thought and discuss it. Say a prayer of thankfulness for your blessings.

Stay at home to read those books you've long intended to read. From your comfortable chair you can send your mind forth on adventure around the world. Discover the pleasure of reading aloud.

Stay home to meditate. Get away by yourself in a quiet room where you can think, undisturbed, about yourself and your destiny. A wise man has said: "We can only be ourselves if we are often enough by ourselves."

Stay home to have fun. Play games in which all can join. Make the house ring with laughter.

Stay home to let go. Drop your cares. Learn the satisfaction of doing as you please. Let time slip by without a thought of the future.

Stay home to find beauty. Open your eyes to a new appreciation of your surroundings: the furniture, the wallpaper, the pictures on the walls, the woodwork, the view from a window, the flowers in the garden...Open yourself to a new awareness of the love in the faces of those with whom your home is shared.

Stay home to relive the past. Revive precious memories. Look at old photographs. Your wedding. Baby pictures of the children. Seek out again the treasures that bind you together as a family.

Stay home to find happiness. Realize the wisdom of simplicity.

Stay home to search for inspiration. Browse through the works of great thinkers, prophets and sages to lift your sights and broaden your vision.

Stay home to prepare for tomorrow, that you may go forth as a new person, with a new spirit, to meet triumphantly the challenges of the outside world.

THE ART OF

Staying Young

he art of staying young depends upon staying youthful on the *inside*, in mind, heart and spirit, in defiance of wrinkles and gray hairs on the *outside*. The Fountain of Youth is *within* you!

Staying young is an *inside* matter. Your body grows old, but your body is not you. "We do not count a man's years," wrote Emerson, "until he has nothing else to count."

Stay young by continuing to grow. You do not grow old, you become old by not growing.

Stay young by hanging on to your dreams. A philosopher writes: "There is not much to do but bury a man when the last of his dreams is dead."

Stay young by maintaining a cheerful attitude. Keep this verse from Proverbs in mind: "A merry heart doeth good like medicine, but a broken spirit drieth up the bones."

Stay young by keeping your mind alive and alert. Scientists have found that the ability to think does not decline with advancing age; the only difference may be a slight decrease in the speed of thinking.

Stay young by forcing your mind out of old ruts. Remember that beaten paths are for beaten men. See new places, read new books, try new hobbies. Increase the depth of your life.

Stay young by remaining flexible, adaptable and open-minded. Do not permit your mental arteries to harden.

Stay young by taking inspiration from the young in spirit who remained creatively active all their lives: Goethe completing Faust at 80; Titian painting masterpieces at 98; Toscanini conducting at 85; Justice Holmes writing Supreme Court decisions at 90; Edison busy in his laboratory at 84; Benjamin Franklin helping to frame the American Constitution at 80.

Stay young by keeping constructively busy. Set yourself new goals for achievement.

Stay young by tackling new projects. The man who planted a tree at 90 was a man of vision. Start ideas and plans rolling that will go on long after you are gone.

Stay young by doing good. Work for worthy causes in your city, state, nation and world.

Stay young by keeping your heart young. "If it can be done," wrote the poet, Carl Sandburg, "it is not a bad practice for a man of many years to die with a boy heart."

Stay young by knowing that "they who wait upon the Lord shall renew their strength; they shall mount up with wings as eagles; they shall run, and not be weary, and they shall walk, and not faint."

THE ART OF
Success

There are no secrets of success. Success is doing the things you know you should do. Success is not doing the things you know you should not do.

Success is not limited to any one area of your life. It encompasses all of the facets of your relationships: as parent, as wife or husband, as citizen, neighbor, worker and all of the others.

Success is not confined to any one part of your personality but is related to the development of all the parts: body, mind, heart and spirit. It is making the most of your *total self*.

Success is discovering your best talents, skills and abilities and applying them where they will make the most effective contribution to your fellow men. In the words of Longfellow it is "doing what you do well, and doing well whatever you do."

Success is harnessing your heart to a task you love to do. It is falling in love with your work. It demands intense concentration on your chief aim in life. It is focusing the full power of all you are on what you have a burning desire to achieve.

Success is ninety-nine per cent mental attitude. It calls for love, joy, optimism, confidence, serenity, poise, faith, courage, cheerfulness, imagination, initiative, tolerance, honesty, humility, patience and enthusiasm.

Success is not arriving at the summit of a mountain as a final destination. It is a continuing upward spiral of progress. It is perpetual growth.

Success is having the courage to meet failure without being defeated. It is refusing to let present loss interfere with your long-range goal.

Success is accepting the challenge of the difficult. In the inspiring words of Phillips Brooks: "Do not pray for tasks equal to your powers. Pray for powers equal to your tasks. Then the doing of your work shall be no miracle, but you shall be the miracle."

Success is relative and individual and personal. It is your answer to the problem of making your minutes, hours, days, weeks, months and years add up to a great life.

THE ART OF
Taking Time To Live

To get the most of life we must take time to live as well as to make a living. We must practice the art of filling our moments with enriching experiences that will give new meaning and depth to our lives.

We should take time for good books; time to absorb the thoughts of poets and philosophers, seers and prophets.

Time for music that washes away from the soul the dust of everyday life.

Time for friendships; time for talks by the fire and walks beneath the stars.

Time for children that we may find again the Kingdom of Heaven within our hearts.

Time for laughter; time for letting go and filling the heart with mirth.

Time for travel; time for pilgrimage and festival, for shrine and exhibit, for rockbound coast and desert, mountain and plain.

Time for nature; time for flower gardens, trees, birds and sunsets.

Time to love and be loved, for love is the greatest thing in the world.

Time for people; time for the interplay of personalities and the interchange of ideas.

Time for solitude; time to be quiet and alone and to look within.

Time to give of ourselves, our talents, abilities, devotions, convictions, that we may contribute to the onward march of man.

Time for worship; time for opening our lives to God's infinite springs of vitality, that we may live more abundantly.

In all ways let us make our moments glow with life. Let us pray as did Matthew Arnold: "Calm, calm me more, nor let me die, before I have begun to live."

THE ART OF
Talking To Yourself

A man thinks in word-symbols, and such silent thought is equivalent to talking to himself. Sometimes when he is alone he speaks the words aloud. But silent or aloud, his conversation with himself is creative...it makes him what he is.

More important than what others say to him is what he says to himself. A man's life is shaped by the way he habitually talks to himself.

A man can talk himself up or down, into happiness or unhappiness, into failure or success, into heaven or hell.

When he talks to himself in words of self-pity, defeat, cynicism, futility, fear, anxiety, despair, hopelessness and resignation, he tears himself apart and shatters his future.

A man can transform his life by switching the emphasis of his inner conversation to words that lift and inspire.

He can talk strength into his backbone so he will have the courage and confidence to stand up to life.

He can talk himself out of discouragement and despair by counting his many blessings.

He can talk himself into accepting hardships and handicaps and enduring them with a gallant spirit.

He can talk himself into seeing his duties and responsibilities in a new light—as opportunities and privileges.

He can talk himself into having a new faith in the love of God and the greatness of men.

He can talk to himself about the beauty, glory and wonder of life so it will glow with a new radiance.

He can talk to himself about his dreams, hopes and aspirations. He can convince himself that there is a place for him and an important work for him to do.

The way a man talks to himself has a dynamic power for self-influence. His words can make or unmake his life.

"Nobody," wrote Cicero, "can give you wiser advice than yourself."

THE ART OF
Tension

There is no life without tension. Evolution is the story of stress and conflict, change and adjustment—the unconquerable urge of life to emerge in new forms.

The philosophy of "easy does it" meets no challenge, records no progress.

Man does not win a race, climb a mountain, write a book, give a speech, paint a picture, develop an invention, found a business, or do anything that matters without tension. Tension quickens the senses, alerts mind and body.

Tension is man on tiptoe reaching for the stars. Tension is the fire of the spirit, the thirst for achievement, the surge of dynamic energy.

Tension is your friend. It is concern, excitement, stimulation, drive. It is you mobilized, applying the best that is in you to the task before you. It is all of your powers organized and concentrated for victory.

Tension has its evil side. When extreme and sustained it often kills. Extreme rest and ease, on the other hand, deadens initiative and extinguishes the creative spark. The secret is this: *Balance tension with rest.*

The Master of men withdrew to mountain, desert and lake to rest, meditate and renew his spirit that he might return with new strength to His great work. He said: "Come ye apart into a desert place and rest awhile."

Every man needs a place of retreat...his own Walden Pond. Thus he recharges himself, so he can be tense again in a good cause!

Tension and relaxation can be instantly balanced even in the midst of action. Close your eyes for a moment and fly away from tension on the wings of imagination...see yourself on the shores of a quiet lake or walking through a sunny meadow. A wise scientist counsels: "Use your moments of unavoidable delay to relax and build up your energy reserves."

By alternating tension and relaxation you balance pressure and release, outgo and intake, giving and receiving, expending and renewing.

Not tension *alone*, not relaxation *alone*, but both in balance is the key to creative living.

THE ART OF
Thanksgiving

The art of thanksgiving is *thanksliving*. It is gratitude in action. It is applying Albert Schweitzer's philosophy: "In gratitude for your own good fortune you must render in return some sacrifice of your life for other life."

It is thanking God for the gift of life by living it triumphantly.

It is thanking God for your talents and abilities by accepting them as obligations to be invested for the common good.

It is thanking God for all that men and women have done for you by doing things for others.

It is thanking God for opportunities by accepting them as a challenge to achievement.

It is thanking God for happiness by striving to make others happy.

It is thanking God for beauty by helping to make the world more beautiful.

It is thanking God for inspiration by trying to be an inspiration to others.

It is thanking God for health and strength by the care and reverence you show your body.

It is thanking God for the creative ideas that enrich life by adding your own creative contributions to human progress.

It is thanking God for each new day by living it to the fullest.

It is thanking God by giving hands, arms, legs and voice to your thankful spirit.

It is adding to your prayers of thanksgiving, acts of *thanksliving*.

THE ART OF
Thinking

The art of thinking is the greatest art of all, for "as man thinketh in his heart, so is he." The thinker knows he is today where his thoughts have taken him and that he is building his future by the quality of the thoughts he thinks.

He recognizes his sovereign control of his own mind and decides what will enter his Mental Kingdom through his sense gateways; he thinks for himself, considers the evidence, seeks the truth and builds his life upon it.

He sets no limitations on the the power of thought; he recognizes that big thinking precedes big achievement.

He creates mental pictures of his goals, then works to make those pictures become realities.

He knows that everything starts with an idea and that the creative power of thought is the greatest power in the universe.

He sees with the "single eye" of intense concentration, seeking facts just as a powerful searchlight penetrates the darkness.

He keeps an open mind, observing, analyzing, considering, questioning—looking for the hidden key which will unlock the problem.

He thinks of his mind as a factory and gives it the raw material, the facts and data, from which ideas are fashioned.

He thinks both objectively and subjectively; he gathers mental power both from the world without and mind within.

He uses the magic power of his subconscious mind, commanding it to come up with ideas while he sleeps; he knows that thought, like a tree, grows night and day.

He studies the laws of cause and effect and strives to work in harmony with them.

He approaches problems both intuitively and logically; he uses the light of his imagination to create and his critical mind to judge; he tests inspiration with logic.

He avoids the one-track mind and sends his mind forth in all directions to expand the range of his mental horizons.

He strives to develop a mature mind without losing the simplicity of childhood.

He creates ideas with humility knowing that behind the idea that he calls his own are the thoughts and efforts of many men.

He realizes that he is at his creative best when he is in tune with the Infinite; when he is open and receptive to the higher powers of mind and spirit.

He exercises his God-given power to choose his own direction and influence his own destiny and he tries to decide wisely and well.

THE ART OF
Tolerance

He who would practice the art of tolerance must guard well against an attitude of superiority, smugness, indifference and coldness. These qualities are tolerance turned wrong side out!

Tolerance is warm. It reaches out the hand of friendship in spite of all differences.

Tolerance is understanding. It is open to new light. He who is tolerant is always eager to explore viewpoints other than his own.

Tolerance is deep. It creates a foundation of faith in humanity underneath disagreements, thus preventing prejudice and resentment. It may reject the argument, but it always respects the man.

Tolerance radiates good will. It disagrees agreeably. It unites men in spirit even though they are a thousand miles apart in their convictions.

Tolerance practices fair play. It doesn't force one man's views on another. The tolerant man makes up his own mind and extends to others the same freedom. He agrees with Josh Billings that "the best creed we can have is charity toward the creeds of others."

Tolerance refuses to hate. Booker T. Washington put it well when he said, "I will not permit any man to narrow and degrade my soul by making me hate him."

Tolerance is sympathetic. It looks through mental barriers into the human heart. It agrees with the French proverb: "To comprehend all is to pardon all."

Tolerance does not look down on others, it looks up to them. Henry Van Dyke gave us a golden maxim for tolerance when he wrote: "Live by admiration rather than disgust. Judge people by their best, not by their worst."

Tolerance towers above differences. It is bigger than race, color, creed, or politics.

THE ART OF
Traveling

When you pack your bags to explore the beauties of your own country or to travel around the world, consider these keys to a happy journey:

Travel lightly. You are not traveling for people to see you!

Travel slowly. Jet planes are for getting places not seeing places; take time to absorb the beauty and inspiration of a mountain or a cathedral.

Travel expectantly. Every place you visit is like a surprise package to be opened. Untie the strings with an expectation of high adventure.

Travel hopefully. "To travel hopefully," wrote Robert Louis Stevenson, "is better than to arrive."

Travel humbly. Visit people and places with reverence and respect for their traditions and ways of life.

Travel courteously. Consideration for your fellow travelers and your hosts will smooth the way through the most difficult days.

Travel gratefully. Show appreciation for the many things that are being done by others for your enjoyment and comfort.

Travel with an open mind. Leave your prejudices at home.

Travel with curiosity. It is not how far you go, but how deeply you go that mines the gold of experience. Thoreau wrote a big book about tiny Walden Pond.

Travel with imagination. As the Old Spanish proverb puts it: "He who would bring home the wealth of the Indies must carry the wealth of the Indies with him."

Travel fearlessly. Banish worry and timidity; the world and its people belong to you just as you belong to the world.

Travel relaxed. Make up your mind to have a good time. Let go and let God.

Travel patiently. It takes time to understand others, especially when there are barriers of language and custom; keep flexible and adaptable to all situations.

Travel with the spirit of a world citizen. You'll discover that people are basically much the same the world around. Be an ambassador of good will to all people.

THE ART OF
Walking

Walking exercises the *whole man*.

Walking exercises the body. It gives the arms and legs a workout. It stimulates the flow of blood; expands the lungs. It is gentle and relaxing.

Walking exercises the mind. It shakes up the brain cells. It fills them with oxygen; drives out the cobwebs. A famous scientist says he does his best thinking on the two miles of sidewalk between his home and his office.

Walking exercises the emotions. It gives you a chance to observe and enjoy the world. Open your eyes to beauty. See the homes, the trees, the gardens. See the shining faces of little children. Listen for church chimes, singing birds and the laughter of happy people.

Walking uplifts the spirit. Breathe out the poisons of tension, stress and worry; breathe in the power of God. Send forth little silent prayers of good will toward those you meet.

Walk with the sense of being a part of a vast universe. Consider the thousands of miles of earth beneath your feet; think of the limitless expanse of space above your head. Walk in awe, wonder and humility.

Walk at all times of day. In the early morning when the world is just waking up. Late at night under the stars. Along a busy city street at noontime.

Walk in all kinds of weather. Experience the glory of earth coming back to life in springtime; the warming rays of the sun in summer; the zest of October's bright-blue weather; the rugged desolation of winter. Walk in the rain and in a blizzard.

Walk alone mostly, but if with a companion, choose one who knows the secret of quietness.

Walk for fun and adventure, for health and inspiration.

And when you go for a walk remember these words by Elbert Hubbard: "Carry your chin in and the crown of your head high. We are gods in the chrysalis."

THE ART OF
Words

The dictionary is full of words. It is how words are *used* that makes the big difference. Words can lift us into heaven or lower us into hell... "Good words anoint a man, ill words kill a man," wrote John Florio.

Words sung in a lullaby can put a babe to sleep; words of hatred and passion can arouse a mob to violence.

Words have both the explosive power of a nuclear bomb and the soothing effect of oil on troubled waters. They can start a war or they can keep the peace.

The art of words is to use them creatively; to select and arrange them to inspire the mind, stir the heart, lift the spirit...

Words of encouragement fan the spark of genius into the flame of achievement. Legend tells us that Lincoln's dying mother called her small son to her bedside and whispered, "Be somebody, Abe!"

Words are magnets that draw back to us the thoughts they express. "Beware, beware!" warned the Hindu mystic. "What goes forth from you will come back to you."

Words are the pegs on which we hang creative ideas. We must put our dreams into eloquent words that others may be persuaded to help us build them into realities. This proverb of Solomon says it well: "A word fitly spoken is like apples of gold in a setting of silver."

Words of faith, hope and courage lift men upward. Negative words drag men downward. "Nerve us up with incessant affirmatives," counseled Emerson; "don't waste yourself in rejection, nor bark against the bad, but chant the beauty of the good. When that is spoken which has a right to be spoken, the chatter and the criticism will stop."

Words are symbols of man's finest qualities. Words such as *valiant, radiant, triumphant, vibrant, heroic*...These are words to live by!

Words are a dynamic force for changing men and nations. Words of power burst in man's mind with a great light, to illuminate his thought and show him the way.

Choose well your words! They will go marching down the years in the lives you touch!

THE ART OF
Work

ork brings man to life, sets him in motion. Work is man in action doing things. Nothing happens until people go to work. Work creates the world we live in.

The right attitude toward work multiplies achievement.

The art of work consists of what you think about your work, how you feel about your work, and what you do about your work.

It is abolishing the concept of work as chains and slavery, and seeing it as freedom to create and build and help.

It is striving to find work you can love, a job to which you can harness your heart.

It is idealizing your work, turning a job into a mission, a task into a career.

It is doing your present work so well that it will open doors to new opportunities. Tasks done at a high standard pave the way to bigger things.

It is glorifying your work, putting a halo around your job.

It is saying with the poet Henry Van Dyke: "This is my work, my blessing, not my doom."

It is discovering the great healing power of work. If you are lonely...work! If you are worried or fearful...work! If you are discouraged or defeated...work! Work is the key to happiness.

It is working with enthusiasm, recognizing with Maxim Gorki that "The game is not only worth the candle, it is worth the whole bonfire."

It is making your work *you*. It is putting the stamp of your unique personality on the work you do. It is pouring your spirit into your task. It is making your work a reflection of your faith, your integrity, your ideals.

It is recognizing that work, not repose, is the *destiny* of man. It is only through work that you can express yourself and make a contribution to human progress.

It is going to your work as you go to worship, with a prayer of thankfulness and the aspiration to serve.

James W. Elliott said it all in nine words: "Work is life and good work is good life."

THE ART OF
Worship

Outer symbols create the atmosphere and mood of worship—the altar, the cross, the candles, the stained-glass windows; the silent sanctuary before the service begins...

In cathedral or cottage, the art of worship is an *inner adventure*; it is the personal practice of the presence of God.

It is meditation and prayer expressing the soul's sincere desire.

It is resting our weary hearts and minds on the Everlasting Arms.

It is emptying and cleansing our minds of fear and worry, jealousy and envy that God may fill the vacuum with His goodness.

It is being quiet and relaxed that we may experience the inflow of the peace that passes all understanding.

It is counting our many blessings and giving thanks for the power to grow, to serve, to conquer ourselves and to discover the sublime values of the life of the spirit.

It is the inspiring realization that this is God's world, that all life pulsates with God's eternal purpose and that we are a part of the divine pattern and plan.

It is envisioning, high and lifted up, all that is heroic, great, good and beautiful in our common life.

It is realigning our lives again with the laws and principles of God, that we may move forward, with our brothers, on the pathway of the King.

It is the renewing of our noblest dreams and aspirations that we may rise above defeat, failure and discouragement and have another try at making the most of our lives.

It is climbing to the spiritual mountaintop of conscious oneness with God that we may light again the candles of our spirits and return as *new men* to the valley and our work.

THE ART OF
Writing Letters

*T*he pen *is* mightier than the sword! The pen in your hand is a magic wand with which you can send joy, hope, love and courage across deserts and plains, over mountains and seas, around the world and around the corner...

Put your words in a letter. Spoken words die on the empty air. Words in a letter endure and can be read again and again.

Tell those you love that you love them—and tell them *now* while they are alive and eager for appreciation and praise. Send them love letters!

When families are scattered in many states, and in foreign lands, hold them together with letters.

Friends tend to fade away through neglect. Keep friendships alive with letters.

If you feel burned up with resentment and anger at someone, tell him off in a letter. Get rid of the venom, get it out of your system. *Then burn the letter!*

Young people need to be constantly encouraged to make the most of their lives. Letters serve as pats on the back to cheer them on.

The book that inspired you. The painting that warmed your heart. The music that thrilled you. Thank with letters those whose toil and devotion have enriched your life.

When someone wins an award, gives a speech, leads a drive, preaches an eloquent sermon, or contributes to the general good in any way, lift his spirit with a letter of congratulation.

The doctor who saved your life, who sat for long hours at your bedside. Write him a letter of gratitude for all he has done for you.

Letters are conveyors of ideas. Do you have a suggestion for your mayor, governor, congressman, senator, or the President of the United States? Don't just think it, for no one can read your mind. Put it in a letter and mail it. Letters make citizens articulate.

Keep a notebook handy in which to jot down thought-starters: experiences, adventures, happenings, good news, quotations, to put sparkle into your letters.

Collect cartoons, snapshots, items from newspapers and magazines that have special significance to people you know. Then tuck them in with your letters.

The coming of the postman is like the daily round of a Santa Claus. Your letters can be gifts to add a new glow to the lives of people.

All you need to write a letter is a pen, a piece of paper and *you*. Get into the envelope and seal the flap!

About the Author

Wilferd Peterson was born in Whitehall, Michigan in 1900. His writing career began in 1928 when he joined the Jaqua Company, a Grand Rapids advertising agency. Beginning as a copy writer, he retired as secretary of the board in 1961. In 1960, his inspirational essays began to appear on the "Words to Live By" page of *This Week* magazine, then a supplement to Sunday newspapers. Letters of praise from admiring readers, including Hubert Humphrey, led to the publication of *The Art of Living*, the first of eight volumes of essays which would sell millions of copies over the next two decades. At age 84, Mr. Peterson received an honorary Doctorate of Humane Letters from Aquinas College. Mr. Peterson spent most of his long life in Grand Rapids, Michigan, and continued to inspire his readers with a monthly column in *Science of Mind* magazine called "The Creative Adventure." He lived well into his nineties and considered life to be a glorious search for peace, good will and the best that is in us all.